Organizing for Good

What it Takes to Achieve Sustainable Excellence

Michael H. Annison

Outskirts Press, Inc.
Denver, Colorado

Organizing for Good
What it Takes to Achieve Sustainable Excellence

V2.0

Outskirts Press, Inc.
http://www.outskirtspress.com

ISBN: 978-1-4327-1585-4 Paperback
ISBN: 978-1-4327-0990-7 Hardback

Library of Congress Control Number: 2007938521

PRINTED IN THE UNITED STATES OF AMERICA

We have reached the limits of the
capability of our current philosophy
and resulting methods of management.
Edwards Deming
Introduction – The Trust Factor, 1994

It is important to aim high precisely
because our imperfect natures drag us down;
otherwise the aspirational pull of our ideals is lost,
and we are defeated at the start.
Anthony Kronman
The Lost Lawyer, 1993

Ideas are the blueprints that we use
to create the world of tomorrow
Edward Cornish
Introduction – The Next Three Futures

Acknowledgements

I very much want to acknowledge the people who have helped shape the ideas in this book.

First and foremost have been Westrend Group clients I have had the opportunity to work with over the last 25 years. Their willingness to share the challenges and opportunities, disappointments and celebrations has been a constant source of learning and excitement for which I am grateful.

Dr. Steve Byrum introduced me to Robert Hartman's ideas some years ago. The work we have done independently and collaboratively stimulated my interest in wanting to write about what it meant to organize for good. Tim Engels has been a colleague and his willingness to comment on early drafts of the book have made it better.

Other people read the book and their comments and observations helped improve the clarity of the writing. These included Pam Moran, Irma Babiak Pye and Peter Fraser – and my wife Patsy who is a wonderful editor and an even better writer.

Members of the Hartman Institute have continued to refine and build on his work. Their ideas, and what Robert Hartman's work means, are reflected throughout the book. I am particularly grateful for the opportunities I have had to listen to, and share ideas with, Dr. Rem Edwards, Wayne Carpenter, KT Connor, Vera and David Mefford, Marcos Gojman – the head of the Hartman Institute in Mexico - and Ron Price. They have individually and collectively contributed to my understanding of Hartman's work. I also want to thank the staff at the Samuel C. Williams Library at Stevens Institute of Technology, the home of Frederick Taylor's papers, and the staff at the Hoskins Library at the University of Tennessee in Knoxville where Robert Hartman's papers are housed.

Finally, my wife Patsy; my daughters Elizabeth and Julia; and now our growing family including their husbands, Jarrod and Garrett, and grandchildren - Annison, Tanner and Reese - are each and all a source of pride and enjoyment.

Finally, every writer should be as fortunate as I have been in having a friend such as Karen Kahlua. In addition to be a respected and effective consultant, she had a masters degree in editing. The book is much the better for her work. Having said that it should be clear that I am still responsible for whatever mistakes or shortcomings remain.

Dedication

For the women in my life

Patsy

Elizabeth and Julia

and

my grandchildren Annison, Tanner and Reese

and 'the boys'

Garrett and Jarrod

Table of Contents

Introduction

I wrote this book, because I believe it is time to rethink how we manage and - more importantly - how we think about management itself.

For almost a hundred years, we have based our approaches to management on the work of a mechanical engineer named Frederick Taylor who summarized his ideas in his book The Principles of Scientific Management published in 1911. Taylor is generally acknowledged to be 'the father' of scientific management and his ideas have shaped the training and behavior of generations of managers. His central thesis was that 'in the past man had been first, in the future the system would be first.' Taylor believed that the problems of efficiency would be solved by developing systems rather than great leaders. Part of his belief in systems was the idea there was 'one best way' to do any job and data were essential to finding that 'one best way.' Like the air we breathe, Taylor's ideas are everywhere, but - also like the air we breathe - they're rarely seen and not often discussed.

Taylor's book, articles and interviews have left an indelible stamp on how today's managers do their jobs. Peter Drucker has called The Principles of Scientific Management "the most powerful as well as the most lasting contribution America has made to western thought since the Federalist Papers;" Social commentator Jeremy Rifkin observed that Taylor "probably had a greater effect on the private and public lives of men and women in the twentieth century than any other individual;" and historian

Anson Rabinbach suggested that "no other development in the history of industrial work had an impact equivalent to Frederick Winslow Taylor's ideas of industrial organization."[1] Many of today's managers may not know who Taylor was but that doesn't diminish the impact he continues to have on how they manage.

Taylor's work almost always generated controversy. Throughout his career, critics argued scientific management was designed to "overwork and enslave men, replace skilled mechanics with drones and cause unemployment."[2] In January, 1912, the United States House of Representatives Committee to Investigate the Taylor and Other Systems of Shop Management began generating testimony that would eventually be transcribed in over 1,400 pages. Congressman William Bauchop Wilson, later the first Secretary of Labor in the Wilson administration, summed up the opposition to Taylor's ideas when he said "we're not dealing with horses nor singing birds but . . . . with men who are a part of society and for whose benefit society is organized."[3] Social critic Upton Sinclair echoed the same themes saying scientific management exploited workers and would lead to a loss of jobs and employment.[4]

The lines of the debate in Taylor's time and our own have been clearly drawn: the question has been whether man or the system would be first. It is essentially an either/or debate: are you in favor of systems or people? All of the related questions about 'hard' and 'soft' management styles, the differences between leaders and managers and debates about whether to focus on customers or employees are cast in this same 'either/or' framework. Managers, consultants, writers and politicians debated whether Taylor was right, but as a practical matter, managers have put the system first. Taylor's ideas have shaped how they were trained and how they manage.

Taylor pioneered the use of time and motion studies and contemporary approaches to quality continue to reflect his emphasis on measurement and data. Innovations such as management by objectives (MBO) discussed by Peter Drucker in his 1954 book <u>The Practice of Management</u>, (1954) Performance Evaluation Review Techniques (PERT Systems) developed in

1957 by the U.S. Navy, Edwards Deming's Total Quality Management (TQM) published in his book Out of Crisis *(1986)*, as well as Six Sigma, lean production, kaizen, and other similar techniques all have their roots in Taylor's work. The tools are more sophisticated but the underlying ideas and principles are the same.

In the introduction to The Principles of Scientific Management Taylor had written that his ideas could "be applied with equal force to all social activities"[5] and over the hundred years since the book was published, they have been. Almost all of us - whether we work in business, on farms or in schools, hospitals, not-for profits or public agencies - implicitly or explicitly make decisions based on Frederick Taylor's ideas. The business consultant/author Gary Hamel acknowledged the impact of Taylor's ideas when he wrote in 2000 that "the 20th century ended pretty much as it began. It began with Frederick Winslow Taylor and the search for efficiency. It ended the same way, with reengineering and supply chain integration and people with promises and charts trying to excise inefficiency where ever they found it."[6]

While Taylor's ideas have had a major impact on how we manage, there are other views that suggest they need to be rethought.

Shortly before he died, Edwards Deming wrote "we have reached the limits of the capability of our current philosophy and resulting methods of management."[7]

I believe Deming, Hamel and others who have made the same point are correct. Mechanical efficiency can never by itself be the basis for sustained excellence. We need to think anew about the meaning of work, what makes people productive and how we manage organizations.

Robert Hartman's ideas about 'organizing for good' are important because they provide a good starting point for thinking differently about how we manage.

By way of background, Hartman was a German whose life spanned the two world wars. He was a child at the outbreak of World War I and a young lawyer and judge in the 1930's prior to the outbreak of World War II. Hartman was one of Hitler's early opponents based on his conviction that Hitler embodied evil. From Hartman's perspective, Hitler was evil – but even more significantly, he was able to organize evil. Hartman's life was spent acting on his conviction that if Hitler could organize evil, there had to be ways to 'organize for good.' His work in the fields of philosophy, economics and business was all focused on the question of what it meant to 'organize for good.'

The differences between Hartman and Taylor are clear:

- Taylor believed 'the system would be first;" Hartman believed people should be first.
- Taylor focused on limiting judgment and the range of decisions workers made; Hartman believed in enhancing judgment.
- Taylor focused on mechanics and efficiency, Hartman focused on meaning and effectiveness.

There are other distinctions as well, but the key point is that Hartman's work enables us to transcend the 'either/or' choices that are implicit in Taylor's work and most contemporary thinking about management. For Hartman, the question isn't whether to focus on people or systems but how people and systems are related and what that means for how we can achieve and sustain excellence.

The Book

The book has five chapters. The first is on Frederick Taylor - his life, his ideas, their impact and why we need to move on. The second is on Robert Hartman's life and work. The third discusses people and 'organizing for good.' The fourth discusses organizations and how they can arranged to achieve excellence by focusing on what it means to 'organize for good.' The final chapter summarizes what it means to manage differently.

The book centers on the importance of judgment – in our personal lives and in our work. It is intended to be a brief practical discussion of ideas that can help us accomplish more than we can by continuing to do what we have done in the past.

I hope you find the book stimulating and - more importantly – helpful.

Part 1

Frederick Taylor and Robert Hartman

Chapter 1

Frederick W. Taylor and Scientific Management

The world was different in 1911: the average life expectancy in the United States was 47 years; 8% of American households had telephones; there were 8,000 automobiles; the average wage was 22 cents an hour; and only 6% of us had high school diplomas.

Fifty years later John Kenneth Galbraith would write a book in which he described the United States as an "affluent society."[8] Galbraith's "affluent society" was a country in which the number of homes with television sets had reached 87% and - in the decade of the 1950s alone - there was a 40% gain in real income, automobile registrations rose by 53% and there were enough new teachers in classrooms to hold 44% more students in the nation's schools.[9] From 1900 to 1950, improvements in the quality of life in the United States and developed nations of the world were extraordinary and Frederick Taylor's ideas about scientific management were the basis for much of the progress. Taylor had applied his ideas to the job; Henry Ford would apply them to the production line and William Durant would apply them at General Motors to create what would become one of the first multidivisional holding companies. Peter Drucker has suggested that one of the greatest, if not the greatest, innovation of the 20th century was the idea of management and that idea has its roots in Taylor's work.

Taylor himself was born to a prosperous Philadelphia Quaker family 2 years before the start of the Civil War. He died in 1915 having lived through a period of remarkable change in the United States.

The American Civil War was the century's great tragic and pivotal event. By the late 1800s people in both the North and South came to think of it as a failure of democracy, culture and ideas. Following the war, it took nearly a half a century for the United States to develop a new way of thinking and a culture strong enough to hold the nation together[10] and, in the late 1800s and particularly after the turn of the century, Taylor's ideas were a significant part of developing that new culture.

Taylor's career spanned the transition from the agricultural society into which he was born to the industrial society his ideas helped advance. We tend to forget that in the late 1800s the United States was still largely undeveloped. The old West was dying, the new industrial society was emerging, but during Taylor's lifetime both were very much alive. At about the same time Taylor went to work at the Midvale Steel Company in Philadelphia, for example, Wyatt Earp and his brothers gunned down the Clancy's in the gunfight at the OK Corral in Tombstone, Arizona.[11]

Beyond the transition from gunfights and agriculture to manufacturing and industry, the period of Taylor's life was remarkable in three ways. First, during the late 1800s and early 1900s, there was an explosion of ideas.[12] In legal circles, Oliver Wendell Holmes emerged as a leading scholar and jurist and his distinctly utilitarian insights helped shape the law. As a lawyer, judge and eventually Chief Justice of the United States Supreme Court, Holmes consistently focused on "the aggregate social good" and had little interest in individuals[13], a theme reflected in Taylor's emphasis on 'the system.' Holmes' views are significant because in many ways they reflected the prevailing ideas of Taylor and what we would consider the elites of the time. In his writings, judicial opinions and comments to friends, Holmes made it clear he distrusted the common man and thought him, as one observer noted, incapable of understanding the political and economic complexities of the time.[14] Like Holmes, Taylor distrusted the common man's ability to manage his work and developed scientific management in part to restrict the worker's ability to make decisions. In science, Louis Agissiz and colleagues helped establish what would become the National Academy of Science. Agassiz's commitment to a scientific approach was based on first observing and second generalizing about what he saw – an approach that over time provided the basis for an emerging view of the social sciences[15] and as well as Taylor's work on time motion studies and cost accounting. There were new ideas in other fields as well. Charles Darwin published the Voyage of the Beagle in 1859; John Dewey was beginning a career as philosopher and educator; and in physics, Albert Einstein and Max Planck were reshaping how we thought about physics, the world around us and the nature of reality. Each of these ideas was individually significant - taken together they provided the context and the stimulus for Taylor's work throughout his career.

Second, the late 1800s and early 1900s was a period of remarkable inventiveness. At the World's Fair in 1876, Thomas Edison displayed his quadraplex telegraph and Alexander Graham Bell demonstrated his telephone. Throughout Taylor's life there was a steady stream of discoveries and inventions that included - as just a partial list - the typewriter (1867), vulcanized rubber (1867), the cable street car (1873), the light bulb (1879), the squeegee window cleaner (1892), the zipper (1893), the radio (1895), the airplane (1903) and the traffic stoplight (1912).[16] Taylor himself held about two dozen patents on products as diverse as car wheels, hothouses, metal cutting devices and even golf clubs. [Like many of us Taylor was a frustrated golfer who wrote in a letter to a friend that 'the ball refuses to settle in the cup, as it ought to, and also in most cases declines to go either in the direction that I wish or the required distance."][17] These developments and thousands of others like them changed our lives and required us to think differently about how we lived and worked.

Finally, the period was a time of upheaval and conflict. There were debates and conflicts about the rights of individuals versus the rights of corporations, as well as conflicts about which branches of government should have what kinds of authority. Taylor's work was near the center of the conflicts over worker's rights.

Early in his career Taylor went to work at Bethlehem Steel where his contributions sound very much like what most of today's managers would like to achieve. As a Bethlehem Steel manager, Taylor:

- developed the capability to analyze output and costs on a daily basis,
- implemented a modern cost accounting system,
- lowered the cost per ton of materials handled from eight cents to four, and
- achieved a two thirds reduction of yard workers - from 500 to 140[18]

He accomplished this by significantly changing the way people worked and was able to achieve cost savings even though he added positions including such as clerks, time-study engineers and supervisors while reducing the staff who actually did the work.

After he left Bethlehem, Taylor worked as a manager or business consultant and served as the President of the American Society for Mechanical Engineers (ASME). He continued to write articles and books and over time distilled the key points of his work in his paper 'Shop Management' published in 1903 and The Principles of Scientific Management published in 1911.

The Principles of Scientific Management

The Principles of Scientific Management was Taylor's defining work. In its opening Taylor said he wrote it for three reasons.

> "First, to point out the losses which the whole country is suffering through inefficiency in almost all of our daily acts;
>
> Second, to try to convince the reader that the remedy for this inefficiency lies in systematic management rather than in searching for some unusual or extraordinary man; and
>
> Third, to prove that the best management is a true science, resting upon clearly defined laws, rules and principles, as a foundation.[19]"

His central premise was "in the past man had been first, in the future the system would be first."[20]

Taylor's work has had – and continues to have – a profound influence on the way people think about management. A personal example: one Saturday while I was writing this book, I took a vacuum cleaner in to be repaired. As I was waiting my turn I watched the woman in front of me trying to exchange a six dollar package of vacuum cleaner bags. The clerk told her she needed a receipt because the computer system wouldn't let them make the exchange without the number on the receipt and, in the words of the clerk, "apparently 'they' (the invisible and omnipresent 'they') don't trust us to handle six dollar exchanges." This is just one example of the idea that the system should be first and workers should not use their judgment to make decisions about what they do; there are numerous others each of us encounters every day.

The approach we use to manage the airline system is an example of Taylor's ideas applied on a global scale. Delta, as they say in their ads, may 'be ready when we are,' but the reality is that travelers have to accommodate themselves to schedules determined by the hub and spoke system used to manage the international air transportation system comes first. The admitting and registration process in the American hospital is another. Automated credit rating systems and the widespread use of automated teller machines are examples of how systems have affected financial services.

Throughout the late 1800s and early 1900s Taylor argued 'scientific management' was essential because traditional production methods that relied on the skills and judgment of individual craftsmen wasted resources. This waste continued because craftsmen passed on their individual ways of working to apprentices who continued to work in the ways their sponsors had taught them. [21] In today's terminology, Taylor was arguing there were no systems and too much variation.

Taylor developed precise job descriptions for his mangers. The purpose was to clarify what they were to do and in so doing reduce the worker's ability to make decisions. His Repair Boss job description reproduced below (with the typographical errors in the original corrected) is a wonderful example of how Taylor defined his manager's duties and controlled workers. There were similar, and equally precise, job descriptions for the: Gang Boss, Speed Boss, Inspector, Route Clerk, Instruction Card man, Time and Cost Clerk and Shop Disciplinarian.

Duties of the Repair Boss	
Superintendent	1-The Repair Boss will report to the Superintendent.
Machines	2-He will see that each workman keeps his machine clean free from rust and scratches.
	3-He will see that all standards established for the care and maintenance of the machinery are rightly maintained.
Lubrication	4-He will see that the machines are properly lubricated.
Belting	5- He will see that all the standards established on belt are rigidly maintained.
Floor	6- He will see that the floors and the yard are kept clean.
	7-He will see that all materials in the shop and yard are piled in an orderly manner and he must bring all disorder to the notice of the Gang Boss, and then if not corrected to the Manager.
Shafting	8-He shall see that all line and counter shafting, loose pulleys, etc. are kept properly lubricated and clean.
General	9-He will report to the Superintendent, verbally and in writing, anything that he may see going wrong.

Taylor's developed four principles that reflected his belief that there was 'one best way' to do any job and he spent his career promoting them.[22]

Principle 1 Replace rule of thumb work methods with methods based on a scientific study of the tasks

Taylor believed scientific study data were essential to efficiency. His own work and the work of protégés such as Harvey Gantt (developer of Gantt charts), Carl Barth and Frank Gilbreth (who with his wife Lillian and their family were the basis for the original book and then the movies *Cheaper by the Dozen*[23]) was all undertaken to find 'the one best way.'

Over time Taylor saw he could improve efficiency by focusing on the job.

This required breaking jobs down into individual tasks, timing how efficiently workers did those tasks and then using the data to find ways the work could be done more efficiently.

His work at Bethlehem Steel was one example of replacing rules of thumb with data. There Taylor concluded that a 'first class man' could only work 43% of the day when handling pig iron (when each pig weighed 92 pounds.)[24] There were similar studies on subjects such as how to shovel coal,[25] produce ball bearings for bicycles[26] and arrange lathes and belts to improve efficiency and increase output.[27]

This first principle has become the basis for how most contemporary managers, regardless of the type of work they do, make decisions.

- Computer manufacturing - In the last 3 months of 1991 Dell Computer produced 49,269 computers; now, according to Shayne Myhand, the day shift manager at Dell's flagship factory, they will "on a good day, during peak demand, exceed that number by lunchtime."[28]

- Fast food retailing – In the fast food business companies know how long it takes a customer – on average – to place their order, pay for it and pick it up - 203.6 seconds. They know Wendy's is 16.7 seconds faster than McDonalds and 21 seconds faster than Burger King. The data are important, because according to industry consultant Jack Sparagowski – who was hopefully exaggerating - "Most chains would sell their first born to get that speed."[29]

- Consumer marketing – companies now routinely use data to anticipate consumer demand for their products. A week ahead of Hurricane Frances's landfall in 2004, Linda M. Dillman, Wal-mart's Chief Information Officer, pressed her staff to come up with forecasts of what Wal-mart stores would need to stock based on what customers had purchased when Hurricane Charley struck several weeks earlier. She believed the company could "start predicting what's going to happen, instead of waiting for it to happen." By analyzing the trillions of bytes' worth of shopper history stored in Wal-Mart's computer network, Dilman found Wal-mart stores would indeed need certain products - but not just the usual flashlights: "We didn't know in the past that strawberry Pop-Tarts increase in sales like seven times their normal sales rate, ... and the pre-hurricane top-selling item was beer."[30]

- Sports – The use of data in sports has been one of the great changes in every sport. In his bestselling book Moneyball, Michael Lewis wrote about the difference between traditional and newer approaches to how the game was managed based on data. Golf fans now know Tiger Woods averages 1.73 putts when he hits the green in regulation, Annika Sorenstam averages 1.75. Woods makes sand saves 54.2% of the time, Sorenstam 59.5%. Woods averages 316 yards per drive, Sorenstam 263. The point is clear: if you have a chance to play with one of them in a pro-am tournament you want Woods to drive, Sorenstam to take the sand shots and either one of them to putt.[31] In auto racing, anyone who has watched the Indianapolis 500 has seen the banks of tires – and computers in every team's pit. In football we now know that going for a first down on fourth and short yardage is, as often as not, a good decision.[32] (It is important in each of these examples to remember that in sports - as in life - timing is everything. Data can be helpful, but timing is key.)

- Agriculture – John Deere uses its 'GreenStar Yield System' to help farmers increase their output. Their combines now monitor as many as 125 variables as they move across the field. Data on soil composition, moisture and a host of other variables are all collected and downloaded to computers to provide farmers with data to help them manage their farms more effectively.[33] Some farmers still have an instinct for the seasons and the land – but all of them have computers.

Every reader can add examples of their own: data are now the coin of the realm.

> "Not everything that counts can be counted, and not everything that can be counted counts."
>
> Albert Einstein

The difficulty is that while data can be helpful, it isn't always clear what they tells you. Dr. Jim Bagian, a former astronaut and presently Director of the National Center for Patient Safety at the Veteran's Administration, makes the point that the number of tickets given to speeders on Interstate 495 around Washington D.C. doesn't tell how many people were speeding – it tells you how many people got tickets. The first problem with data is being clear about what they are actually measuring. A second problem is what the data actually mean. The drop in murder rates in many American cities probably tells us as much or more about the effectiveness of paramedics and their ability to get to crimes scenes and save victims as it does about a reduction in people trying to kill each other. The third problem is understanding that while the data may be quantitative, it may not be objective. Robert Parker's wine ratings have a significant impact on wine sales, but the reality is that very few people can tell the difference between a wine rated 89 and another rated 90.[34] Finally, the data may not measure what matters. Jake "The Snake" Plummer, one time quarterback for the Denver Broncos football team, has passing statistics that in some categories are better than John Elway's. Elway's numbers may not be as good as Plummer's, but in the category that matters most Elway comes out ahead; it is Elway, not Plummer, who has two Super Bowl rings.

While data is important and can be useful judgment about what it actually means is essential.

The point is data may be helpful but never substitute for good judgment.

Principle 2 Scientifically select, train and develop each worker rather than passively leaving them to train themselves.

Taylor's intent was to eliminate the need for the worker to make decisions about what they did and instead to "do what they were told and do it quick."[35]

To accomplish this, Taylor introduced the idea of the 'task.' Essentially, Taylor's task idea meant work should be fully planned at least a day in advance and managers should give the workman written instructions detailing what he was expected to do, how he was to do it and the time it was to take.[36] Taylor wrote that the "workman who is best suited actually to do the work is incapable (either through lack of education or through insufficient mental capacity) of understanding this science"[37] and therefore needed training and direction.

Taylor's managers were expected to develop these instructions so that one sheet would have a list of the tools the worker would need and another a history of his previous day's work. Yellow sheets showed the man he had not done his work up to standard; white indicated he had performed satisfactorily.[38] The dashboards, benchmark reports, process studies, and blizzard of paperwork that now threatens to swamp us all are all the logical – an in many cases excessive - extension of these simple sheets Taylor developed in the early 1900s.

Principle 3 Cooperate with the workers to insure that the scientifically developed methods are being followed.

Taylor wanted his managers to support and cooperate with their men, because he believed it would make the men more efficient. As a practical matter, he was interested in their 'arms and legs' and what they could do rather than their 'hearts and minds' and who they were. His approach reflected the same utilitarian view Oliver Wendell Holmes took toward the law.

While he was interested in what his men could do rather than who they were Taylor's views were inconsistent. He routinely referred to himself as 'one of the men' but in reality had nothing in common with the men he supervised. Taylor had spent his youth traveling in Europe, received his education at one of the country's most exclusive prep schools and throughout his life had homes in the most affluent sections of whatever town in which he happened to be living. He was a good tennis player and had won the Men's National Tennis Doubles Championship (1881).[39] The men who worked for him didn't live the way Taylor did and never would.

At the same time, he had a strong sense of justice and believed workers should share in the benefits of his system. He was committed to the idea that the increased income that resulted from the implementation of his system should be shared by the owners and the men who actually did the work. These conflicts about who should benefit from increased efficiency are still with us today.

Principle 4 Divide work nearly equally between managers and workers, so the managers apply scientific management principles to planning the work and the workers actually perform tasks.

Over time, Taylor became increasingly fond of talking about

what it meant to be a good worker – a worker he described as a 'high priced man.' His example was a man named Henry Noll whom Taylor - for the purpose of his stories - renamed 'Schmidt'. In those stories, Taylor said he asked Schmidt if he was a 'high priced man' – and then went on to tell him a 'high priced man' 'will do exactly as this man tells you to-morrow from morning to night. When he tells you to "pick up a pig and walk, you pick it up and you walk, and when he tells you to sit down and rest, you sit down. You do that right straight through the day. And what's more, no back talk."[40]

> "And what's more,
> no back talk."
> Frederick W. Taylor

While the words are usually more tactful, this approach is not all that different from how some managers behave today.

A Note on Taylor and Financial Management

Taylor's work on financial management bears mentioning because, while less well known, it is every bit as important as his work on scientific management. Robert Kanigel, one of Taylor's biographers, has gone so far as to suggest that even without his work on scientific management, Taylor's contributions to financial management and cost accounting would have secured his place in history.[41]

Taylor's approach to financial management was striking in its simplicity: he developed ways to measure the relationship between time and money. Prior to this work, there was no such thing as cost accounting as we think of it today. By 1895 Taylor had a consulting practice and the stamp (business card) he had made to advertise his business stated "Systematizing Shop Management and Manufacturing Costs a Specialty."[42] In putting a cost to what was done and how long it took, Taylor set the stage for future developments that have become increasingly sophisticated.

Now almost a century later, Taylor's work on financial management and cost accounting was deemed to be "a basis for all modern industrial accounting."[43] When we refer to 'cost-benefit' analysis we are referring to updated variations of Taylor's at the start of the last century. Continuing work in the fields of finance and economics and the ability to use computers to manipulate staggering amounts of data have led to increasingly sophisticated applications of Taylor's original ideas. The applications in both the practical world – with developments such as activity-based accounting – and the academic world are more sophisticated than in Taylor's time, but as with the refinements of scientific management, the core ideas are essentially the same.

Taylor's Impact

In The Principles of Scientific Management, Taylor suggested his ideas could be applied to every area of society. He was remarkably prescient in that over time his ideas were in fact widely adopted in the United States and more broadly by organizations and governments around the world. His impact was even more remarkable because of the way in which his ideas came to public attention.

It's a wonderful story.

While Taylor was known within his own field he was not widely known until Louis Brandeis – the future Supreme Court Justice – coined the phrase 'scientific management' and brought Taylor's work to national attention. The publicity Taylor and his ideas received during the Eastern Railroad Rate Case hearings in 1910 was the tipping point in his career.

Prior to the hearings, Taylor had been a manager and a consultant with a record of mixed results. After the hearings, he was an international celebrity and plausibly the first of what we might now think of as superstar consultants. Tom Peter's 'skunk camps' of the 1980s[44] were a direct descendent of Taylor's lectures and seminars conducted at his home 60 years earlier.

In June 1910, Congress passed the Mann-Elkins Act, which required railroads and other common carriers to obtain rate hike approval. Soon after the legislation passed, the Interstate Commerce Commission (ICC) created by the legislation opened hearings on railroad rates at the Waldorf Astoria hotel in New York City. Louis Brandeis represented groups opposed to the rate increases. Shortly after the hearings began, Brandeis realized the railroad executives had no idea what their actual costs really were. During the hearings, for example, he asked James McCrea, President of the Pennsylvania Railroad, if he knew that the costs the railroad paid were what they should have been; McCrea responded by saying "I do not know, quite, how I can answer that." Charles Daly, a New York Central Vice President, responded that based on his experience the costs were not unduly high. When Brandeis asked if there was any basis for his answer other than his 'arbitrary judgment', Daly answered "None whatever."[45]

> And finally we propose to show the huge field for the application of scientific management in American Railroad operation and the rich fruit in economies and improved service which may be expected to result.
>
> Louis D. Brandeis, Taylor Collection, Williams Library, 1911,

Brandeis had a flair for showmanship and during the hearings the New York Times ran the headline:

Railroads Could Save
$1,000,000 a Day

Brandeis says Scientific Management
Would Do It – Calls
Rate Increases Unnecessary[46]

To put Brandies' comment in perspective, it would be the equivalent today of saying today that a small group of large companies – say computer companies or automobile makers - could save one billion nine hundred thirty million dollars

($1,930,000,000) every day[47] – something close to four hundred billion ($400,000,0000,000.00) dollars a year. Brandeis got people's attention and the resulting publicity made Taylor an international celebrity. The result was that managers in every part of the society scrambled to install what they understood was scientific management and the impact - as Gary Hamel pointed out - is still with us today.

Education

In education, Taylor's ideas began to influence school systems across the country. Frank Spaulding, the superintendent of schools in Newton Massachusetts completed a study using Taylor's scientific management and cost accounting techniques that showed that "5.9 pupil recitations in Greek are of the same value as 23.824 recitations in French; 12 pupil recitations in science are equivalent in value to 19.2 pupil recitations in English; and that it takes 41.7 pupil recitations and vocal music to equal the value of 13.9 pupil recitations in art." There was no longer a need for judgment about the relative value of different fields of study; decisions about what to teach could be made by applying scientific management and Taylor's cost accounting system.[48]

Health Care

Taylor's emphasis on data and 'one best way' was reflected in the work of Dr. Ernest Codman. Codman graduated from the Harvard Medical School in 1895 and completed his internship at the Massachusetts General Hospital. He joined the surgical staff of the hospital and became a member of the Harvard Faculty, seemingly destined for a career as a respected successful physician.

Codman did, however, have convictions about how medicine should be practiced that created debates that are still with us today. Simply put, Codman believed that physicians should use data (Taylor's scientific management) to assess the quality of their medical practice and report the results to their patients.

His idea was not well received. Codman lost his staff privileges when Massachusetts General refused to institute his plan. After losing his privileges, Codman opened his own hospital. His approach was based on the use of data and a hospital register to help physicians improve the quality of care they provided. Over time, Codman's "end result system of hospital standardization"[49] became the goal of the American College of Surgeons and his work on quality assessment was a forerunner of standards developed by what is now the Joint Commission on Accreditation of Health Care Organizations (JCAHO).

International Applications

One of the striking aspects of Taylor's work was the extent to which his ideas – for better and worse – were embraced and aggressively promoted by governments – particularly fascist and totalitarian governments - around the world. In 1927, Benito Mussolini promoted Taylor and Taylorism through Fascist Italy. The Principles of Scientific Management had been translated into Italian in 1915 and by 1926 the government had established a propaganda arm to advance Taylor's ideas. In Russia, Lenin and Trotsky both embraced Taylorism; Lenin writing that 'we must introduce in Russia the study and the teaching of the Taylor system and its systematic trial and adaptation.' Taylor's ideas were applied to the management of Nazi concentration camps during World War II and continued to be embraced after the war. Ditlev J. Peukert wrote that the 'unquestioning endorsement [by German delegates to international conferences] of economic efficiency as the highest goal and scientific management as the best means strikes later readers as abstract, austere and almost dehumanized.'[50]

It was the same in other fields as well. A woman named Martha Bensley Bruere fussed about scientific management and suggested that while 'systematizing the household' didn't seem to be something you could 'reduce to an equation' she went on to do just that by advising readers of her books on how to do it. The paper "Scientific Management in American Protestant Churches" by Peter B. Peterson was an example of Taylor's work applied to religion.[51]

Taylor's scientific management could help advance the quality of life around the world. It could also, as in the case of Fascist Italy, Totalitarian Russia or Hitler's Third Reich, be used to advance evil. This reality is one the reasons we need to focus on how to define excellence and what it means to organize for good.

Time to Move On

While acknowledging the positive impact of Taylor's work, there are compelling reasons we need to think differently about how we manage.

The World Has Changed

There are significant practical differences between our world now and the world of 1911: life expectancy is now 77.2 years,[52] over 60% of United States residents have a telephone, the average wage is $34,064,[53] and the literacy rate is estimated at 97%.[54] Further, there are now more than six hundred billion – that's billion with a 'b' - web pages and more than 50 million blogs.[55] We are now overwhelmed by the data Taylor said we needed.

There have been other changes in how we understand the world as well. Some writers have talked about them as 'Megatrends' - the shift from an industrial to an information society,[56] others the shift from an analog to a digital world;[57] or the shift from a world dominated by ordered structures and rules of physics to a world best understood by the

> Let's start with the brutal honesty. Managing, or administering, businesses doesn't work today."
>
> Mike Hammer
> Rich Kallgard, ASAP Interview,
> Forbes Magazine

metaphors of evolutionary biology.[58] Still others have focused on the changing responsibilities of government reflected in the trend toward privatization or changing relationships between various levels of government.[59] These observers have also talked about changes in organizational structure from centralized to decentralized arrangements or - in the case of Charles Handy's observations - the development of the 'cloverleaf organizations.'[60]

There have been changes in organizational life as well. Only one of the companies on the original Dow Jones Index is still on it: General Electric. Wal-mart has now become the world's grocery store chain, Costco is the country's largest seller of wine and, as this is being written, Google and Ebay have (in 2006) a market capitalization larger than General Motors.

However we describe it, it is clear the world in which we live has changed and that means how we manage – and how we think about scientific management -has to change.

Declining Effectiveness

The second reason we need to move on is that Taylor's ideas have been pushed to the extreme and are now often counterproductive. One example is that our preoccupation with data has now probably gone too far. British sociologist Anthony Giddens wrote that "Quantophrenia [quantitative mania] is rife in American sociology departments. For many sociologists, if you can't count it, it doesn't count."[61] Giddens was writing about sociology, but the point applies to us all.

> We spend increasingly larger amounts of energy for increasingly minimal results.
>
> Leanne Kaiser Carlson

A second example has to do with energy and effectiveness. The futurist Leanne Kaiser Carlson points out that in almost every organization, we spend increasingly larger amounts of energy for increasingly minimal results: we work harder and harder and accomplish less and less.[62] Stress and 'burnout' – a word that didn't exist in 1911 – have become a common phenomenon.[63] According to one Wall Street Journal article, accountants are leaving the field because of the hours and pressure of work. Jim Walsh, a human resources manager for PricewaterhouseCoopers, goes so far as to question whether the business model accounting firms have traditionally used still works.[64] The problem isn't confined to accounting. Workplace stress is estimated to cost 300 billion dollars ($300,000,000) each year in missed work and in one survey 62% of the respondents workload has increased over the last 6 months and 53% say work leaves them 'overtired and overwhelmed.'[65]

The frustration with the emphasis on systems also shows up in how some executives view management. Daniel Grossman, who owns and runs Wild Planet Toys, says it this way "if your aspiration is to be a bureaucratic infighter, you may be well suited for a large organization, but you have to swallow more than I care to. On some level you can't be who you really are during the workday."[66] The country western group the Dixie Chicks talk about the loss of meaning in the music business:

> "We listen to the radio to hear what's cookin'
> They sound tired but they don't sound Haggard
> They got money but they don't got Cash."[67]

The difficulty is that, like the body builder who has overtrained and become muscle bound, our organizations have focused on efficiency and increasingly sophisticated applications of Taylor's ideas. As a result they have become obsessed with mechanics and lost sight of the meaning of what they are doing. As one friend observed some years ago, 'we have become so focused on the ants at our feet that we don't see the elephants coming over the hill.'

Most of us want to do a good job and be able to take pride and satisfaction in what we do. Robert Hartman provides a way to move beyond our obsession with mechanics and think about what we do differently.

Chapter 2

Robert S. Hartman and Axiology

Robert Hartman was one of the fortunate ones.

During World War II millions lost their lives; others like Hartman's friend Viktor Frankl were put in concentration camps.[68] Throughout his career, Hartman would talk about the fact that his life was shaped by war and the time and circumstances of his birth. In his lectures and speeches he would point out that he "was raised in Germany. . . born on January 27 in 1910 in Berlin – on the emperor's birthday. . . on the very street which housed the war ministry, Bendlestrasse.[69]

Like Taylor, Hartman was well educated and well traveled. He attended the German College of Political Science, studied law at the University of Paris and attended the London School of Economics and Political Science. In 1932 he got his Bachelor of Laws degree from the University of Berlin and began to teach. In his early twenties, he worked as an assistant district court judge and became active politically. In the early 1930s, he spoke at rallies for the Social Democrat Party, the party opposing Hitler, and wrote articles for Das Freie Wort – the Free Word – attacking the Nazis in general and Hitler specifically.[70]

Because of his outspokenness and writings, the Gestapo came for him. He took the name Robert Hartman because it was the name on a randomly chosen passport he used to flee Germany on June 6, 1933.[71] He would use the name the rest of his life - keeping the middle initial 'S' for his birth name Shirokauer.

After his escape Hartman went to work in England for the Disney Corporation. In the 1930s he told Walt Disney, then the active Chairman of the company, there would be war in Europe; while Disney initially disagreed he did shut down operations in the Scandinavian countries and in the process reassigned Hartman to Mexico and Central America.

Following the war, Hartman began to focus on what would become his life's work. The experiences of war led him to believe that if it was possible for Hitler to organize for evil – not just to be evil but organize evil – it had to be possible to organize for good. This idea consumed him and Hartman would spend his professional life studying, writing and teaching about what it meant.

Hartman initially turned his attention to the law because, as he would later write, he believed the "law would show me what was right and wrong; it would help me organize good as the Nazis were organizing evil."[72] He soon became disenchanted when he reached the conclusion the law could tell him what was legal or not legal but could not tell him what was right or wrong.[73] This conviction eventually led him to conclude he could do more to 'organize for good' through teaching and consulting, which he did for the rest of his life. Over the course of his career, Hartman taught at The Ohio State University (1948-1956) and served as a visiting professor at various colleges and universities including the Massachusetts Institute of Technology (1955-1956), Yale University (1966) and the University of Tennessee. By the end of his teaching career, he had held more than 50 lectureships in the United States, Canada, Latin America and Europe. He died of cancer at 63 in September 1973. (At the time of his death Hartman's wife reported that he had been nominated for the Nobel Prize in 1973 - the year Henry Kissinger and Le Doc Tho received the prize for ending the Vietnam War)[74]

Like Taylor, Hartman was committed to the scientific method, but his work reflected a richer understanding of both the value and limits of scientific inquiry. Taylor was an engineer, Hartman was a philosopher and the difference was evident in how they viewed science and their use of the scientific method. The scientific method had helped Taylor understand and organize work; Hartman would use it to understand and organize goodness.

For Taylor, the "system was first;" for Hartman, people came first and systems had value to the extent they advanced individual well-being. In Hartman's view, human motivation rather than scientific management was the key; the primary factors for human motivation were based in values and judgment rather than economics and money.

Organizing for Good: Judgment and Axiology

A thing is good if it had all the properties it is supposed to have.

To understand how to organize goodness Hartman believed he had to first understand what was goodness. His work in the field of axiology - the study of values and how we make value judgments - led him to the understanding that "a thing was good if it had all the properties it is supposed to have."[75] A table, for example, was a good table if it had legs and a surface. A person was a good person if they were what they were supposed to be. A table that couldn't stand would be less good; as would a person who made decisions based on what other people thought rather than his or her own values and judgment. In this definition, the focus was on the extent to which a thing was what it ought to be. It was explicitly not on whether a person went to church, what they read or how they voted.

Value Tendencies, Judgment and Decisions

Hartman's approach to organizing for good led him to focus on judgment and how we make decisions. His work led him to the conclusion that judgment was the result of the interaction of three dimensions of experience: systemic, extrinsic and intrinsic.

Systemic Value and Valuation

The systemic dimension reflects our thinking self and involves intellectual and abstract mental realities. Examples:

- Mathematical formulas such as "A=L x W" (area equals length times width) are systemic. R x T = D (rate times time equals distance) is another.
- An architect's blueprint, the teacher's lesson plan, a physician's protocol and a recipe are all similarly systemic.
- The ability to see patterns and understand abstract infrastructures and relationships is systemic as well. Business operating systems, financial systems and organizational charts are all systemic.

The systemic dimension has to do with our ability to understand patterns and ideas. By itself the systemic is interesting, but it is useful to the extent that it is the basis for action that helps people. Ideas without action have no impact.

Hartman's point was that while the systemic is important, a preoccupation with it can be counterproductive. He anticipated Edwards Deming's observation on the need for a new theory of management when he wrote in the 1950s that: "we can't live without system, but we can overdo it."[76]

Extrinsic Value and Valuation

> "The only thing that changes this world is taking action."
> Jody Williams, Recipient
> 1997 Nobel Peace Prize

The extrinsic involves the practical dimension of our lives. It is the dimension of day-to-day practicalities and decision making. It is also the basis for comparisons and judgments we make about the extent to which things are what they should be.

In our conversations about organizational life, the extrinsic is what we are talking about as 'corporate culture' or 'how we do things around here.' The extrinsic matters because it reflects how managers think about employees, how professionals set standards and how we think about the responsibilities of leadership.

Intrinsic Value and Valuation

The intrinsic is the human and infinitely unique dimension of who we are; it is, in Hartman's view, our reservoir of strength.[77]

The reason every decision we make has an intrinsic dimension is that everything we do affects people. From Hartman's perspective no decision could be purely extrinsic; there could never be a part of our lives that was 'just business'.

Organizations and their leaders get in trouble when they ignore the intrinsic and think about what they do as 'just business,' a perspective that has - not surprisingly - led to all kinds of problems throughout the public, private and not-for profit sectors.

Hartman's intrinsic, extrinsic and systemic dimensions are apparent in every part of our lives.

Work, for example, can be viewed as:

Systemic	Extrinsic	or	Intrinsic
A Cog in a System	A Job		A Calling

We can view work systemically - something we do because we need the money it provides. This is the Taylor view of work; men are motivated by money and work because they need it. In Taylor's view, the men who work for him are cogs in the system and work itself has no meaning or intrinsic value.

Work can also be viewed extrinsically - something that gives us satisfaction - or intrinsically as a calling - a reflection of who we are and what matters to us. People who are exceptionally good at what they do may use different words to describe it – athletes talk about being in 'the zone.' Business leaders may talk about it differently, but in the end, it is clear that people who talk this way see their work as a calling and an expression of who they are.

Similarly, leadership can be systemic, extrinsic or intrinsic;

Systemic	Extrinsic or	Intrinsic
Thinking	Task oriented	Servant
Planning		Leadership[78]

Most of us have had experience with systemic leaders – these are the people who have ideas but have difficulty implementing them or understanding how they affect people. Similarly we know extrinsic leaders – the task oriented, hard drivers who are focused on the work with little regard for what it means or how they treat people in getting done what needs to be done. Finally, there are intrinsic leaders - people who have systemic and extrinsic strengths but are fundamentally people oriented in their approach to how they manage.

Douglas MacGregor's classic study – The Human Side of the Enterprise – described these differences in terms he coined as Theory X and Theory Y. MacGregor's Theory X leaders assume people inherently dislike work and must be coerced to do what they are supposed to do.[79] This was Taylor's manager with their yellow and white sheets. Theory Y leaders assume people like work and view it as natural as play and rest.

Relationships can be thought of in the same way;

Systemic	Extrinsic or	Intrinsic
Relationship	Network	Friend

The concept of a relationship is inherently systemic. When people go beyond talking about relationships and talk more specifically about relationships at work or in the family, they are beginning to talk about the extrinsic and intrinsic. Extrinsic relationships are what we are talking about when we talk about 'networks' - practical useful relationships that are beneficial in terms of getting something done such as finding a job or getting a promotion. When we talk about friendship, we are talking about the intrinsic and who people are rather than what they can do for us. In an extrinsic relationship we are interested in people for what they do and how they can be useful. In an intrinsic relationship we are interested in people for who they are and in their well being rather than our own.

Balance and Strength

Hartman believed that organizing for good meant we had to understand balance.

The first aspect of balance is balance within each of the three dimensions. For Hartman this meant not over or undervaluing people, practicalities or systems.

Intrinsic Balance

When we overvalue family members, children for example, we spoil them. I have a granddaughter and grandson to whom I am devoted - in Hartman's framework I overvalue them. At the other extreme, undervaluing children means ignoring their needs or, in the extreme, abusing them.

Managers who have strong intrinsic tendencies tend to overvalue people. When they conduct annual evaluations, they tend to rate their people 'above average.' In the case of one client organization that uses a 5-point rating system, managers rated 32% of their employees '5' – the top of scale. 37% were rated '4' – above average, 29% were rated '3' – average, 1% were rated '2' and none were rated '1'.[80] The difficulty comes when managers rate all their employees above average (like the children in Garrison Keilor's Lake Wobegon) above average and organizational performance is average or below. Managers who are intrinsically out of balance are always nice people, but their behavior leads to lower standards, poor performance and increasing confusion.

Managers who undervalue people are at the other extreme. Al 'Chainsaw' Dunlap's career at Sunbeam, Scott Paper and the other companies he managed reflected this undervaluing of the intrinsic and a disdain for people, a point he made clear in his book Mean Business when he wrote 'if they (people who worked for him) want friends let them get a dog."[81] Richard Boynton the head of Sunbeam's household products division described early sessions with Dunlap: 'It was like a dog barking at you for hours, he just yelled, ranted, and raved. He was condescending, belligerent, and disrespectful.''[82] Dunlap's obsession with finances and the stock price of his companies – the extrinsic – led to the ruination of the companies he led and the ongoing pain for the people who worked for them. When Dunlap was fired, employees cheered.

Extrinsic Balance

People who overvalue the extrinsic are hard workers focused on day-to-day responsibilities and tasks. These people are driven: their solution to most issues is to do more of what they are doing. 'Burnout' and the inability to balance the work and personal sides of their lives are common phenomenon among people who overemphasize the extrinsic.

At the other extreme, people who undervalue the extrinsic tend to be casual about practical day-to-day realities. They are slow to respond to phone calls, ignore deadlines or miss budgets. These are the people who make decisions based on intrinsic or systemic tendencies and, as a result, undervalue the extrinsic practical side of what they need to do.

Systemic Balance

Taylor's scientific management and approach to 'his men' is an example of overvaluing the systemic. People who overvalue the systemic tend to get caught up in planning and often have difficulty carrying out their plans – a problem Taylor had throughout his life. Like absent-minded professors they have great ideas but can't follow through. Their organizations tend to have good plans and poor performance.

At the other extreme, people who undervalue the systemic are caught up in unproductive flurries of activities – they are busy but not effective. These people have lists of phone calls to return and equally long lists of things to do but it is not clear that the phone calls or what's on their lists is connected to a clear overall purpose. These people are busy, but it's not clear what they are doing matters.

The second aspect of balance has to do with balance across the three dimensions.

Many of us are strong intrinsically and extrinsically and less strong systemically. This means we care about people and are willing to work hard but may not always see the systemic implications of what we do. Another pattern is one in which executives value people and systems more than the practicalities of getting things done. These are leaders who have great ideas but can't implement them.

The important point about understanding balance among the dimensions is that their relative strength shapes how we make decisions. If we are pressed to make a decision quickly, we will make it based on our strongest value tendency. If our strongest tendency is the extrinsic, we are likely work to harder rather than figure out a better way to do whatever needs to be done. If we overvalue the intrinsic, we are likely to commit to people before considering the impact of what we have decided. The more time we have to consider a decision, the more likely we are to make a balanced judgment because we have time to consider the issue from all three perspectives.

Hartman's concept of balance is important, because organizational leaders always make decisions based on legitimate conflicting interests. These will include conflicts between: needs of individual units and needs of the organization as whole; the present and the future (do we spend now or build the balance sheet?); and, on a third dimension, conflicts between organization and the people it serves. In each case Hartman insists balance is essential and we consider the impact of what we decide on the people our decision will affect.

> Hartman believed Taylor had it backwards: if we were to be effective over time, people had to be first and systems had to be designed to meet their needs.

Hartman was aware of Taylor's work on scientific management. His summary of it was that if the worker was "no more than a bundle of fragmented elements it [was] not possible for him to put his heart and soul into his work."[83]

Hartman developed a schematic that makes it easier to understand the differences between he and Taylor and how the dimensions relate to each other. In the schematic the flag represents the systemic, the circle represents the extrinsic and the cone represents the intrinsic.

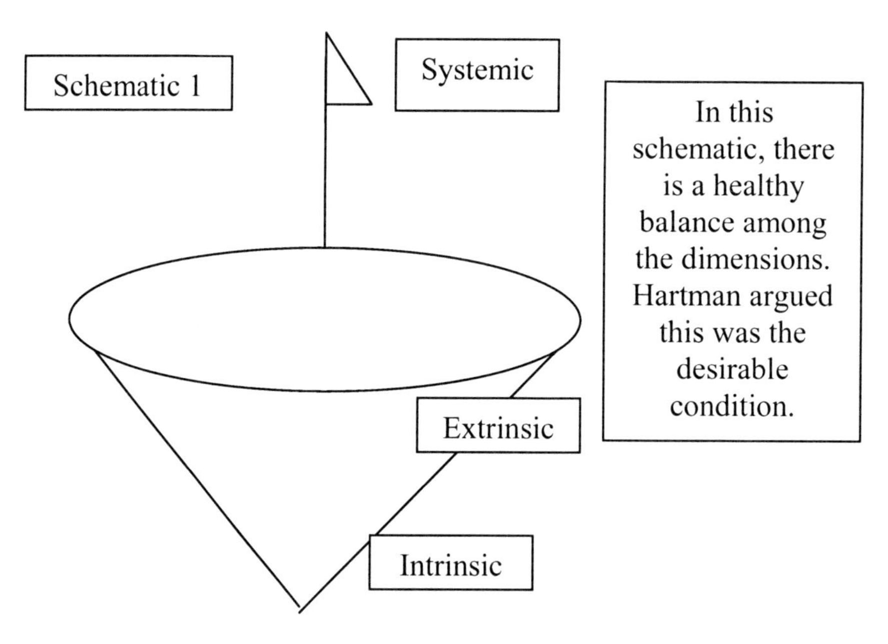

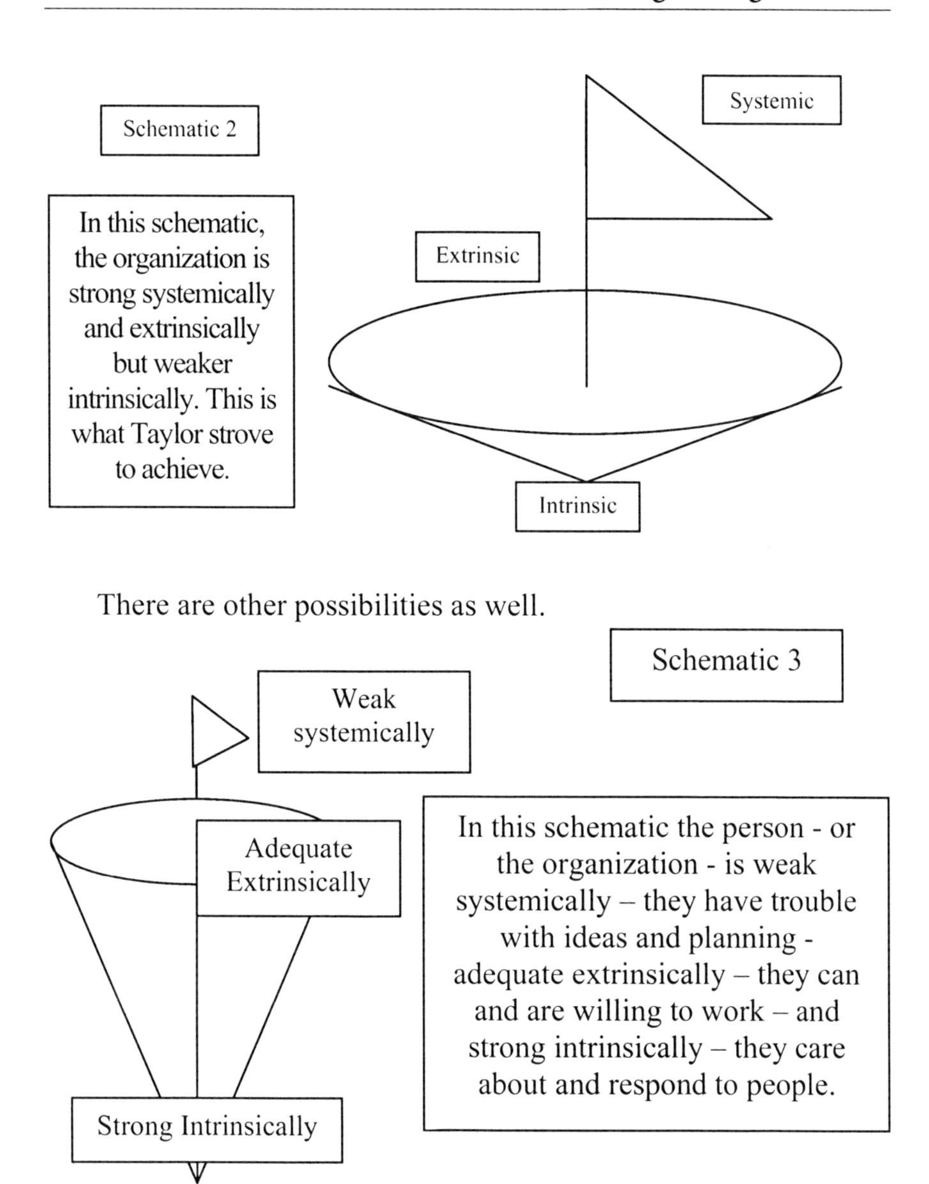

Hartman believed that without a focus on the intrinsic there will always be problems because we will never be fully human -

and in turn the organizations we create will be flawed and fall short of what they could achieve. His belief that "man had developed lopsidedly, that his knowledge of the world has dangerously outstripped his knowledge of himself . . . he has learned how to value and control nature but not how to value and control himself.[84] The companion point is equally clear – the systemic and the extrinsic are essential –but valuable only to the degree they support the intrinsic.

The Hartman Value Profile

During the 1960s, Hartman began to work on ways to assess what it meant to organize for good. He was convinced his work had to have a scientific basis if it was to be useful and accepted.

The development of the Hartman Value Profile was one of the results of this approach.

> "In order to actualize moral values in the world we absolutely need an instrument of clear, intellectual thought that will make these values transparent to everybody."
> Robert Hartman

The Profile is distinctive because it focuses on value tendencies and judgment as the basis for how we make decisions. Other instruments assess issues such as thinking styles (the Myers Briggs),[85] how we approach decisions (the DISC)[86] or emotional intelligence (the work popularized by Daniel Goleman).[87] Hartman's contribution was to develop an approach to assessing judgment that is reflected in attitudes and behavior. Hartman's point is value tendencies shape thinking styles, how we make decisions and our emotional intelligence.

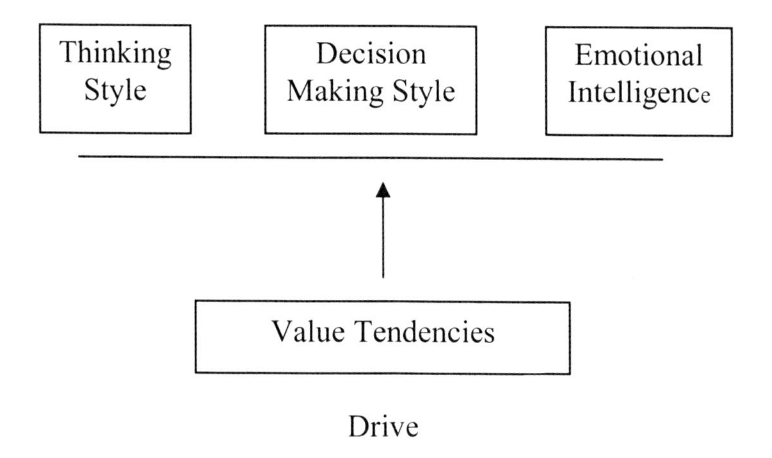

Hartman's belief was if we could understand our own value tendencies, as well as the value tendencies of colleagues and the organizations we have created - we could gain insights that would enable us to organize for good and become more effective. The Profile provides insights about how we value the systemic, extrinsic and intrinsic – and additional insights into issues such as how we value work and the extent to which we are comfortable with change.[88]

Hartman's Value Profile is worthwhile because it helps each of us gain insight into how we make decisions. It is equally valuable for organizations because it provides insights that affect their performance.

Striving for Goodness: Four Rules

Rule 1 - Know Yourself
Rule 2 - Choose Yourself
Rule 3 - Create Yourself
Rule 4 - Give Yourself

Hartman went on to develop four rules to clarify ways to strengthen our judgment. The rules build on one another as parts of a journey toward self-actualization and in this sense there is a kinship with Abraham

Maslow,[89] one of Hartman's contemporaries and friends.

Rule 1- Know Yourself - developing good judgment requires we know ourselves and understand what animates our behavior.

> Too many of us end up bobbing like corks in an ocean going whichever way the wind and the waves take us rather than purposefully pursuing a direction based on knowing who we are.

Whether it is through insights gained via instruments such as the Hartman Value Profile or by taking time to think about our lives, who we are and what matters to us, knowing ourselves is essential to being fully human.

Rule 2 - Choose Yourself[90] – holds we should accept who we are.

Hartman developed the two sets of characteristics that helped clarify the choices we need to become and accept who we are. One set describes what Hartman called 'the man of faith' and the second describes what he called 'the man of fear.'[91] In his consulting work and lectures to managers Hartman presented the two sets of attributes and encouraged managers to assess themselves on each scale to see where they had opportunities to grow.

Hartman's Leadership Assessment

Intrinsic Faith	Intrinsic Fear
Humility	Defiance, spitefulness, superiority
Serenity	Aggressiveness, combativeness defensiveness
Cooperation	Competitiveness
Expansiveness	Restrictiveness, narrowness

Humanness	Cynicism
Magnanimity	Sanctimoniousness, holier than thou
Generosity	Greed
Unpretentiousness	Vanity
Not easily hurt - Equanimity	Touchiness - easily hurt
Boldness courage	Cowardice
Forgiveness	Vengefulness
Light touch	Heavy touch
Uncomplicated - purity	Complicated – lack
Innocence common sense	of common sense
Relevance - Sense of proportion	Irrelevance - no sense of proportion
Rationality	Irrationality
Spontaneity flexibility	Rigidity
Perseverance - patience	Inconsistency - hesitation – impatience
Awareness - Vision - warmth	Myopia – dullness
Compassion	Indifference

The closer we come to having the attributes of the man of faith, the more likely we are moving toward becoming fully who we ought to be.

<u>Rule 3 - Create Yourself</u> – each of us must create ourselves.

The challenge to create ourselves is often a source of confusion – especially for managers who believe they have their jobs because of what they know – the extrinsic – rather than who they are and what they're willing to learn – the intrinsic. Creating ourselves, personally and professionally, means we have to continue to grow and learn. Creating ourselves means we need to think about questions such as:

- what will I be doing five years from now?
- what am I doing now that I will not be doing five years from now?
- what will give me satisfaction?
- what will I have learned?
- what frustrates me now that will no longer frustrate me?

Whether we respond from the perspective of our personal lives or our work, creating ourselves means knowing who we are, accepting who we are and being willing to explore who we can become.

Rule 4 - Give Yourself – Hartman's fourth rule was we should give ourselves.

People and organizations that focus on their own well being rather than serving others will invariably get themselves into trouble.

Hartman went on to suggest ways we could develop ourselves and move towards goodness.

1. Through crisis – we can grow through difficult experiences that force us to look inward and find our strengths.
   Most of us have, at one time or another, been through difficult times; the question is whether or not we have learned from the experience. Similarly, most of us know people who have been through difficulties and become better for it. We also know others who have gone through difficulties and learned nothing. Warren Bennis and Robert J. Thomas have suggested this capacity to learn from personal difficulty is one of the predictors of true leadership. It is, as they put it, the

ability to "learn from even the most trying circumstances."[92]

2. Conscious effort – this is the work we do to learn more about ideas and how the world works (the systemic); it is the work we do to develop our capabilities (the extrinsic) and, even more importantly, the work we do to learn more about ourselves (the intrinsic). Every manager faces the same dilemma - what they need to know is forced on them either by colleagues, professional associations, vendors or clients. For most managers, it is usually harder to take the time to think about what they don't know that they should know or will need to know to be as effective in the future as they have been in the past.

3. Follow the example of sensitive people - this is the opportunity to learn more from people who embody qualities we would like to see and ourselves. They may be people we know or people who are more publicly known; the question is what we can learn from them.[93]

4. Moral development – this is the path of learning more about ourselves and who we are. It may come through crisis, reflection, experience or meditation, but however it comes, moral development is essential if we are to embody the goodness Hartman describes.

5. Peak experience – these are experiences Abraham Maslow described as the times when we feel at our best – at the peak of life. For an athlete, it is the phenomenon of being 'in the zone;' for others of us it is the moments in a relationship, or times at work or even at times when we are alone that we are most aware of who we are and all we can become.

Hartman's rules are designed to help us avoid what the poet David Whyte describes when he talks about getting so caught up in 'busyness' that we lose ourselves in a whirlwind of events that make it harder to remember what we were trying to accomplish, why it matters or who we are.

Hartman's Legacy

Robert Hartman's work is important because it responds to Edwards Deming's point about the need for a new management philosophy.

As we begin a century, it is clear there is now more to be gained by thinking through what it takes to achieve excellence and organize for good than there is from continuing to put our energy into increasingly sophisticated refinements of scientific management.

We have opportunities to improve.

The quality of the products we make can get better. Our focus on 'the system being first' has been valuable but is becoming less effective. Warranty Week – The Newsletter for Warranty Management Professionals – points out that warranty costs are going up – companies produce increasing numbers of flawed products. The top 50 warranty providers reported 22 billion dollars in warranty claims in 2005 – up from 2004.[94]

The quality of services we provide can get better. The difficulties of accounting firms, for example, have been daily newspaper fodder and there is the humiliating example of H&R Block, the company that advises people on their taxes, being unable to file its own corporate tax returns correctly.[95]

Finally, professional ethics and behavior can get improve. The focus on the system rather than people has led to abuses.

It was Albert Einstein who pointed out "You can never solve a problem on the level on which it was created." If we continue to focus on 'the system being first,' we will see more of these problems. To get beyond them we have to think differently about achieving excellence, people, organizations and how we manage.

Part 2

Organizing for Good: The Next Best Way

Chapter 3

People: Organizing for Good

While people like Hartman, Drucker and Einstein left Germany, others stayed. Albert Speer was one of those and his career is one of the best examples of why organizing for good matters. Speer and Hartman were contemporaries, but while Hartman devoted his life to organizing for good, Albert Speer went to work for Adolph Hitler.

Speer was born in 1905 and decided, like his father and grandfather, to become an architect. In 1931, he attended one of Hitler's speeches and came away greatly impressed. Following the speech, Speer joined the National Socialist German Workers Party - the Nazis - and became member number 474,481.[96] Years later Speer wrote in his autobiography that at 28 he was "wild to accomplish things" and would have sold his soul to do it. [97]

He did.

After joining the Nazis, Speer rose rapidly. In the early 1930s, he was a volunteer architect, by 1933 he was salaried. Shortly later he became Hitler's personal architect[98] and in 1942, at the age of 37, he became Germany's Minister of Armaments and Munitions. By the end of the war, it became apparent Speer had been second only to Hitler. He is generally thought to have been responsible for enabling Germany to fight World War II 2 years longer than might otherwise been possible: a point underscored by General F. L. Anderson who commented just before the Nuremberg Trials if he had "known what this man was achieving, I would have sent out the entire American Eighth Air Force merely to put him underground."[99]

Speer was brilliant but had no understanding of the meaning of what he was doing. In his autobiography, written during his 20 years in prison following the end of the war and the Nuremburg trials, Speer wrote that before 1944 he almost never "found the time to reflect about myself or my own activities . . . . I never gave my own existence a thought."[100] This lack of introspection violated Hartman's first rule to 'know yourself.' It was this imbalance of judgment – brilliance in the world of plans and work and the inability to think what he did in terms of its impact on people – that led to Speer's advancing the evil Hartman opposed. The first sign that Speer had any understanding of what he had done was his decision to plead guilty at the Nuremberg trials. He alone among the members of the German high command accepted responsibility for his actions.

On April 9, 1944 the London Observer editorialized that:

> Speer is, in a sense, more important for Germany today than Hitler, Himmler, Goering, Goebbels, or the generals. In him is the very epitome of the "managerial revolution."
>
> Speer is not one of the flamboyant and picturesque Nazis. Whether he has any other than conventional political opinions at all is unknown. He might have joined any other political party which gave him a job and a career. He is very much a successful average man, well dressed, civil, non corrupt, very middle class in his style of life, with a wife and six children. Much less than any of the other German leaders does he stand for anything particularly German or particularly Nazi. He rather symbolizes a type which is becoming increasingly important in all belligerent

> countries: the pure technician, the classless bright young man without background, with no other original aim than to make his way in the world and no other means than his technical and managerial ability. It is the lack of psychological and spiritual ballast, and the ease with which he handles the terrifying technical and organizational machinery of our age which makes this slight type go extremely far nowadays . . . this is their age; the Hitlers and the Himmlers we may get rid of, but the Speers, whatever happens to this particular special man, will long be with us.[101]

The editorial was remarkably prescient. Following World War II, management skills became increasingly important throughout the developed nations. At the same, time people wanted to forget the horrors of the war.

This belief in the importance of management combined with a lack of introspection was a common theme in novels of the late 1940s and early 1950s. William Whyte described the business counterpart of Albert Speer in his 1956 book the The Organization Man[102] - the best selling story of the lives of executives who ran the large organizations that developed after the war. For Whyte, the organization man was simply another interchangeable part of the organization. In words that echo the Observer editorial White wrote that "these people may work for The Organization, they are the ones of lower middle class who have left home, spiritually as well as physically, to take the vows of organization life, and it is they who are the mind and soul of our great self perpetuating institutions."[103]

These organization men were, as ITT's Chairman Harold Geneen put it some years later, "as predictable and controllable as the capital resources they must manage."[104] Geneen believed a good manager could manage any business. His organizing principle was that since management skills were technical (extrinsic), any manager could run any business. Frederick Taylor's "good man" of 1911 had evolved into Albert Speer's technocrat of the Second World War and William Whyte's organization man of the 1950s.

Hartman's Four Questions

Hartman was concerned about this lack of introspection and suggested there were four questions each of us had to answer to be able to become fully human and organize for good.[105]

Question 1 - What am I here for in the world?

This is the intrinsic question.

Who am I? What is it I ought to be doing to enrich the world in which I live? What can I do to contribute to others? In Taylor's world, the question is nonexistent. For Hartman the question is central. The difference between people who do their jobs adequately and others who are outstanding is that, as often as not, the people who are outstanding are doing what they ought to be doing to be fully themselves: they enjoy and care about what they do. This may sound fanciful, but Steve Jobs, Chairman of Apple Computer, made the point clearly in a 2005 graduation speech at Stanford University when he commented on some of the difficult times in his career by saying: "I'm convinced that the only thing that kept me going was that I loved what I did. You've got to find what you love."[106] This love of work isn't restricted to senior successful executives.

Scott Gutstein is an example of someone who loves his work. Gutstein is an 'egg man' at the Flamingo Hotel in Las Vegas. The 'egg men' are the people (men and women) who produce the thousands and thousands of omelets and egg dishes served to guests at buffets provided by Las Vegas hotels. It is a pressure-packed, demanding job. Gutstein was a 'college boy'' who says he 'just found myself' as a egg man.' The work is hectic and hard - and he loves it.[107]

Question 2 - Why do I work with this organization?

This is the extrinsic question.

Organizing for good means we should be doing work consistent with our values. People who work in organizations whose values conflict with their own will be untrue to both themselves and the organization and, as a result, both the organization and the employee will be dissatisfied. Dissatisfied employees usually end up staying with the company and contributing less and less or leaving or being asked to leave.

> I bleed Dodger blue and when I die, I'm going to the big Dodger in the sky.
> Tommy Lasorda

Some examples: Tommy Lasorda, the former manager of the Los Angeles Dodgers, used to say "he bled Dodger Blue." When Phil Knight, the Chairman of Nike, replaced William Perez as the president of the company, Knight said the decision had been difficult before he concluded there was a 'cultural canyon' between Perez and the company. Knight was talking about what Robert Hartman would have described as differences in judgment and value tendencies. Perez was replaced by Mark Parker, a 27 year Nike veteran, who commented when he took the job that "This is more than a job for me. I have a deep connection to the brands and the company."[108]

Question 3 - What can this organization do to help me fulfill my meaning in the world?

This is the systemic question that encourages us to view the organization as a vehicle to help us accomplish what we need and want to do.

For Taylor, the system (and the organization) was the end in itself; for Hartman the organization is the means to an end. From a personal standpoint, the goal is to find work that enables us to become fully who we ought to be, the result of which is essential for us and valuable for the organization. Example: Martin Rosenblum, the corporate historian for Harley Davidson, says he works for the company 'because it has soul.' Making motorcycles is basic manufacturing and assembly work, but Harley has found ways to infuse it with meaning.

Question 4 - How can I help this organization to help me fulfill my meaning in the world?

This is the overall question that enables each of us to fulfill ourselves and in so doing fulfill our duty to the organization; the organization becomes the creative instrument of our own self fulfillment.

Hartman's four questions encourage us to think differently about work. Each of his questions focuses on who we are and what we can do to become fully ourselves rather than how we can build networks to get ahead at something we may or may not want to do. The questions apply to each of us regardless of what we do.

People Who Do the Work

In 1959 Frederick Herzberg published The Motivation to Work based on the results of a study he and colleagues had undertaken to answer the question "what do workers want from their jobs?"[109] Herzberg and his colleagues identified what they called 'motivators' - those factors that were important to people in their work and 'hygiene' factors - those factors that were necessary but not motivators. Herzberg identified five key motivators:

1. Achievement

   When workers described what motivated them, Herzberg and his colleagues usually heard stories of achievement centered around a job or work completed.

2. Recognition

   Almost one third of the workers in Herzberg's study

talked about recognition from supervisors, peers, customers or subordinates.

3. Work Itself

   Aspects of the job that gave workers satisfaction. Workers cited creative or challenging work and the opportunity to do a job completely from beginning to end.

4. Responsibility

   > "Most of us are motivated by intrinsic rewards: interesting challenging work, and the opportunity to achieve and grow into greater responsibility."
   > Frederick Herzberg, 2002

   Responsibility included the opportunity to work without supervision, becoming responsible for the work of others or taking on additional responsibility even without formal advancement.

5. Advancement

   Advancement, in many cases unexpected.

There were additional factors,[110] but these five were the principal motivators. For Herzberg – who used essentially the same words Hartman would use several years later - the motivators were the intrinsic factors; the hygiene factors were extrinsic. His distinction was the motivators had to do with the job itself and hygiene factors had to do with the job situation. The extrinsic factors - the conditions of work - had to be acceptable but would not in and of themselves motivate people to accomplish what needed to be done or go beyond putting in their time.[111]

Herzberg's findings made the same point that had come out of the Elton Mayo's experiments at the Western Electric Hawthorne Works in Chicago. Between 1924 and 1927[112] Mayo and his colleagues changed the sequence, length and timing of rest periods, dismissal times and piece-work arrangements for a selected group of women. The key finding was no matter how the working conditions were changed the women's output rose.

From the Hartman perspective the lesson is clear: regardless of the changes they experienced, the women believed they were valued and, as a result, they responded to each change by doing as much or more than was asked of them.

Taylor's views were consistent with McGregor's Theory Y and reflected in his comments about 'soldiering' – the practice of workers deliberately doing less work than they were capable of doing.[113] In Taylor's view soldiering was pursued with conscious intent.

> The natural laziness of men is serious, but by far the greatest evil from which both workmen and employers are suffering is the systematic soldiering which is almost universal under all of the ordinary schemes of management and which results from a careful study on the part of the workmen of what will promote their best interests.[114]

For Hartman the focus has to be on the person: the Hawthorne experiments and Herzberg's motivators – while they predate Hartman's work – are good examples of his ideas. Taylor's approach might produce gains in the short term but will never be effective over time - a fact reflected in Leanne Kaiser Carlson's observation that we are now working harder and harder to accomplish less and less.

Hartman encourages us to focus on who people are rather than what they do.

Hartman encourages us to understand when human beings are seen through the lens of their work—what they do as opposed to who they are — the person is devalued; their performance suffers and the organization is less effective that it could be.

The lesson is clear: organizing for good and creating the next best way means we have to think differently about how we treat people we serve, people who do the work and people with whom we work.

Professionals: White Collar Privileges and Responsibilities

In 1912 Louis Brandeis gave the commencement address at Brown University. In his address, Brandeis suggested business people should be considered professionals and went on to describe what he saw as three defining characteristics of professionals and a profession:

> First. A profession is an occupation for which the necessary preliminary training is intellectual and character, involving knowledge and to some extent learning, as distinguished from skill.
>
> Second. It is an occupation which is pursued largely for others and not merely for one's self.
>
> Third. It is an occupation in which the amount of financial return is not the accepted measure of success.[115]

Over time the emphasis on scientific management and efficiency, rather than effectiveness, has affected professionals and they have drifted away from the characteristics Brandeis described. The pressures inherent in rising client expectations, demands to improve productivity and changes in traditional payment arrangements have led to changes in how professionals think about Brandeis's three points.

Learning and Knowledge

The challenge for professionals to keep up with what they are supposed to know is increasingly difficult.

First, professionals are expected to master knowledge within their own profession – a responsibility that has become increasingly difficult because of constantly increasing volumes of information being produced. One example: The Atmospheric Radiation Measurement (ARM) Program publishes 150 refereed articles per year. This means a professional in the field would have to read three a week to cover them all. In other professions, the number of publications and articles is much higher. During the writing of this section, I Googled 'professional articles accounting' and got over 50,000 titles in .11 of a second.

Most fields have subspecialties, so the challenge to keep up is compounded by increasing amounts of information being generated by sub-specialists in fields that continue to develop further subspecialties. There are all kinds of examples of this growth of subspecialties. We now have 'financial gerontology', forensic accountants and psycho-historians, along with a growing number of subspecialties in every other field as well.

The point is clear: there is more and more for professionals to know and it is harder for them to keep up. In the 1980s I worked with John Naisbitt and Jeff Hallet at the Naisbitt Group. In what seems the distant past, we used to talk about being 'gutted with data and starved for intelligence.' The phenomenon is more true now than it was when we talked about it then.

Second, professionals are expected to be increasingly knowledgeable about the context within which they do their work. The doctor is expected to stay current on: a) developments within his or her own field; b) public policy and what it means for how they practice; c) the financial implications of clinical decisions they make; d) issues related to organizational change and its affect on how they practice medicine; and e) the impact of emerging technologies and how to manage technological innovation.

These pressures are compounded by an insistence on speed. This insistence on doing more faster reduces the time the professional (whether they are a doctor, lawyer, accountant, architect, engineer or a professional in any other field) has for their clients. Laureen Stiller Rickleen summarized the challenge for lawyers when she observed that she 'sees a lot of people who are distressed about where the profession has gone. They don't like being part of a billable hour production unit. They want more meaning out of their lives than that."[116]

The not surprising result is frustration for the professional who wants to do a good job and dissatisfaction for the client who feels they are being rushed through the system. As the actress Carrie Fisher observed: "The problem with Americans is that even instant gratification takes too long."

Pursued for Others

Scientific management turned our attention inward toward how we managed work and the organization and, not surprisingly, this has affected the judgment of professionals. Too many end up focusing on efficiency and professional expectations rather than the well being of people they serve. Two examples. First, in The Organization Man William Whyte posed what he himself said was a silly problem. It was the following:

A middle-management executive is in a spot of trouble. He finds that the small branch plant he's helping to run is very likely to blow up. There is a way to save it: if he presses a certain button the explosion will be averted. Unfortunately, however, just as he's about to press a button his boss heaves into view. The boss is a scoundrel and a fool, and at this moment he's so scared he is almost incoherent. Don't press the button, he says.

The middle-management man is no rebel and he knows that the boss, stupid as he is, represents The Organization. Still, he would like to save everyone's life. Thus his dilemma: if he presses the button he will not be acting like a good organization man and the plant will be saved. If he doesn't press it he will be a good organization man and they will all be blown to smithereens.

A second example:

> In his book on the media James Fallows described the following discussion that occurred on a public television program. A panel of reporters was given the following hypothetical situation:

Each was to think of himself – they were all men - as a reporter embedded with a group of enemy guerilla soldiers fighting against the United States. In this capacity they see a group of American soldiers walking into a guerilla ambush. The question is whether the reporter should warn the troops.

Dan Rather, the retired CBS news anchor angrily maintained the reporter should not warn the soldiers because 'he was a newspaperman with a professional responsibility.'[117] The generals on the panel expressed disgust that the people who represented the media they were fighting to defend could take such a cavalier attitude toward a soldier's life.

In both cases, the conflict is between the extrinsic demands of a profession and intrinsic responsibilities we have as human beings. The difficulty is when the extrinsic becomes the dominant framework because people get hurt and professionals behave badly.

- Professional Wall Street money managers persuaded United Airlines to move employee pension funds from bonds to riskier investments in stocks. The retirees lost their money, but the professional money managers got paid.[118]

- One Wall Street securities analyst was reported to have traded favorable coverage of selected stocks for a million dollar contribution to a an especially competitive New York City kindergarten to which he wanted to be sure his children would be admitted.[119] Money that should have gone to employees, shareholders or customers went to promote one individual's selfish interest.

- A Boston physician left a patient on the operating table in the middle of an operation while he left to go to his bank several blocks from the hospital.[120] The demands of his personal life outweighed Brandeis's idea of service to others.

In too many cases the response is either 'it's just business,' 'everyone does it' or 'that's just the way we do things around here.'

The common theme in these examples and others like them is usually hubris - overbearing pride or arrogance - greed - an excessive desire to acquire more (of anything) than we need - or a combination of them both. During the trials of the Enron Chairman and President, the company's former chief financial officer provided a contemporary example of Albert Speer's problem and the London Economist's prescience when he said in court that he had 'lost his moral compass.'[121] Neither hubris or greed is appropriate if we agree with Brandeis's observations about professionals or Hartman's ideas about organizing for good have merit.

While there are abuses, it is important to be clear there are also examples of professionals focusing on the people they serve and doing what's right. Ethan Berman, Founder and Chief Executive of RiskMetrics, a private company spun off from J.P. Morgan, wrote the chairman of his Board's compensation committee requesting he 'receive no increase in salary, zero stock options, a smaller bonus than last year and a piece of the company's profit sharing pie equal to that received by all employees."[122]

The practical side of getting things done is obviously important. The difficulties come when the concern for extrinsic practicalities leads to people being hurt or badly served.

Measures of Success

Some professionals have ignored Brandies' comments about how to measure success and have focused on making money rather than serving clients.

- The former head of one of America's leading insurance companies made millions by operating on the principle that all he wanted was 'an unfair advantage.'[123]

- Some professionals receive salaries that many consider outrageous. In cases such as the former head of the not-for-profit New York Stock Exchange, the question is whether the job was worth the salary and a 140 million dollar retirement package.[124]

- In numerous other examples, the question is whether corporate executives commit fraud to become eligible for stock options and bonuses.

Neither Brandeis nor Hartman was against people making a good living – they were opposed to greed before service and money before people.

> Most issues facing business leaders are, in the final analysis, questions of judgment.
>
> Warren Bennis and James O'Toole

Some observers have written thoughtfully and insightfully about how we got into these situations and what can do to do better in the future. Warren Bennis and James O' Toole have written about how 'business schools lost their way.'[125] Their argument is business schools have focused On the 'scientific model' and lost sight of the fact that business is a profession rather than a trade. In effect, business schools embraced Taylor's argument that management was a 'true science.' This belief is true, but only partially. There is a place for scientific management, but knowing how to manage systems will always be just a part of a manager's responsibility. At a broader level, management will always be about people. Managers may benefit from insights gained through the scientific method but that doesn't make business a science. Garison Keillor once observed 'you could no more become a Christian by going to church than you could become a car by standing in the garage.'[126] The analogy applies to management: using data doesn't make it a science. Bennis and O'Toole make it clear by adopting a scientific model as the basis for their curriculum business schools focused on abstractions (the systemic) rather than the realities of what professional managers do.

In the same vein, Anthony Kronman, the former Dean of the Yale law school, wrote about the impact of these issues on lawyers. [127] Kronman suggested there was a "spiritual crisis" that affected the legal profession and the crisis was the result of the demise of a set of values which were based on the understanding that a good lawyer was "not simply an accomplished technician but a person of prudence or practical wisdom as well."[128] In writing about the importance of restoring professionalism to the legal profession, Kronman argued that it is "the intrinsic judgment, not expertise, that counts and it is this quality of judgment the ideal of the lawyer statesman values most"[129] The words echo Hartman and make the point that a preoccupation with the extrinsic is as hurtful to lawyers as it is to the people on the assembly line, managers and executives.

If, as Robert Hartman defined it, a thing is good to the extent that it is what it ought to be, the issue is to be clear about what organizing for good means for professionals; how they think about what they do and how they behave.

> Technical competence is both desirable and necessary but will never by itself be the basis for distinction.

Leadership

Hartman's comments about leadership provide a unifying framework for much of what has been recently written about leadership.

- When Stephen Covey talks about 'Principle-Centered Leadership' he is talking about the intrinsic side of leadership. [130]
- One of Warren Bennis's many wonderful stories about leadership includes a discussion of why members of the Boston Philharmonic Orchestra respect their conductor Seija Ozawa. When Bennis asked orchestra members why

they liked Ozawa the response he got was Ozawa "didn't waste their time." Ozawa understood the importance of showing respect and it was reflected in how he managed their time.[131] Talking about respect, Zarin Mehta, founder of the Bombay Symphony, observed "The days of someone saying, 'Shut up and play' are over."[132]

- James MacGregor Burns's discussions about transformational leadership,[133] Jim Collins writings about Level 5 Leadership,[134] James O'Toole's books about values [135]and Margaret Wheatley's observations about relationships and 'the new science of leadership'[136] all emphasize the importance of the intrinsic side of leadership.

Other writers have emphasized the importance of the extrinsic and systemic.

- Ram Charan, a management consultant and Larry Bossidy, the Chairman of Allied Signal, write about the extrinsic practical side of management in Execution: The Discipline of Getting Things Done.[137]

- Michael Porter has written about excellent execution as a reasonable strategy for any organization. For Porter, "Operational effectiveness and strategy are both essential to superior performance, which is the primary goal of any enterprise."[138]

- Henry Mintzberg writes about the systemic aspects of leadership when he talks about schools of planning.[139] Mintzberg identifies 10 different schools and depending on individual organizational circumstances each has value.

Hartman's work is distinctive because it provides a unifying framework for these ideas. His ideas help us transcend the 'either/or' approaches that have characterized much of what is being written; the choice isn't between

- people and systems but how to arrange people and systems effectively; just as
- 'hard' and 'soft' management styles but rather how to achieve a discipline that recognizes people's worth and enables them to be effective.

In the Hartman framework each writer's contribution is part of the whole. The schematic summarizes how the work of each writer reflects the dimensions of Hartman's framework. The extrinsic and systemic dimensions have merit to the extent they support the intrinsic

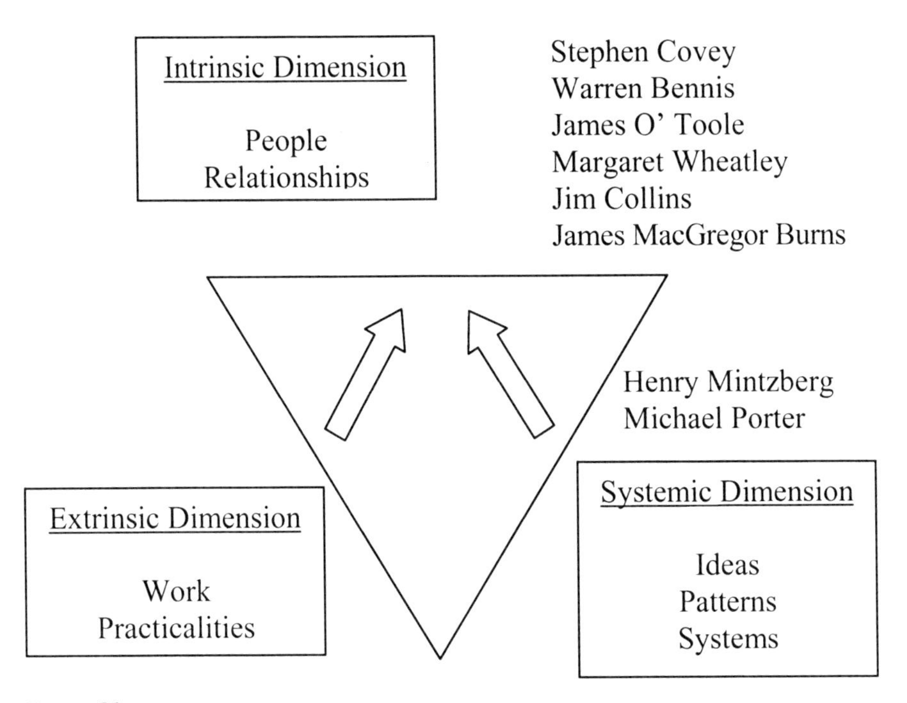

A second focus of recent work on leadership has focused on distinctions between managers and leaders. The starting point for much of what has been written was an article by Abraham Zaleznick in the Harvard Business Review in 1977.[140] Zaleznick's central point was that managers reacted while leaders were proactive. Others such as Harvard's John Kotter[141] have refined ideas about the differences between leaders and managers but it was Zalesnick's pioneering article that introduced the issue as it is generally understood. Management as they and others describe it, has to do with work and tasks; leadership has to do with people and managing change and the future. Taylor's description of what his managers would do (instruction card clerk, time clerk, inspector, traditional gang boss and shop disciplinarian)[142] is in the category of what we would now think of as managing.

More recently, Marcus Buckingham and colleagues at the Gallup Organization suggested a different way to think about management. Buckingham's point is managers and leaders both exercise judgment and make decisions that affect the organization and its future. The old saying that says 'managers do things right and leaders do the right things" no longer makes sense: leaders and managers both have to do the right thing and they both have do it well.

A more useful way to distinguish between leaders and managers has to do with the scope of their responsibilities and the nature of the issues with which they.

The key difference has to do with differences in the time frame and scope of issues for which they are responsible.

Judgment matters at every level of the organization. What differentiates workers, managers and leaders is their capacity for systemic thinking and the ability to arrange extrinsic practicalities to support people.

Research on differences in value tendencies among people at different levels of responsibility suggests a basic intrinsic capacity is essential for success at all levels. As people advance to middle management, the distinguishing characteristic of success becomes the ability to think systemically – an ability to grasp overall patterns and systems. Further advancement assumes this capacity for systemic thinking and requires even strong intrinsic capacities.

From Robert Hartman's perspective the requirements then become clear.

- Manage the Intrinsic - People
  This capacity includes two qualities: the ability to deal with people effectively and an understanding that the key to the organization's success is the ability to attract, recruit, select, place, evaluate and develop people.

- Manage the Extrinsic - Culture
  Leaders recognize the importance of clearly establishing 'how we will do things around here.' They design operating systems and influence how people in the organization work together and treat each other.

- Manage the Systemic - Vision
  Leaders articulate a sense of the possible that inspires people and to which people are willing to commit their energy. Buckingham described this as the ability to identify what binds groups of people together rather than what distinguishes them.

- Maintain Balance – Manage Change
  Finally, leaders manage change and balance their commitment to the organization and its people with the ability to assess it objectively to see how it needs to improve or change.

When Hartman talked about leadership, his point was "the higher you go in management the more essential becomes the use of your inner self, your spiritual power, because your decisions become increasingly loaded with moral and spiritual implications"[143]

Hartman's points about leadership were reflected in a 2006 presentation Doris Kearns Goodwin made in Denver. She described Lincoln's leadership attributes and the traits she described included empathy – what she described as Lincoln's ability to reach people's hearts; his willingness to assume responsibility for his decisions: a commitment to sharing credit and the capacity to learn from mistakes and change his mind based on new facts. The striking thing about the list is the extent to which the qualities reflect Hartman's ideas of balance.

Organizing for good doesn't eliminate the dilemmas William Whyte and Jim Fallows described – nor does it eliminate the conflicts and challenges managers deal with every day. It does make them more manageable because it provides a way to think clearly about how to make appropriate decisions. The manager in the plant pushes the button to save people's lives and the embedded reporter puts his or her intrinsic responsibilities to save the lives of the soldiers, above the extrinsic responsibilities of the profession.

In the final analysis, the responsibility of the leader is to ensure this focus on people underlies all that is done in planning or in the practical day-to-day work of the organization.

Chapter 4

Organizing for Good

Every organization faces challenges. The issue is to be clear about what they are, how we have approached them in the past and how the idea of achieving excellence and organizing for good can help deal with them effectively in the future.

Frederick Taylor believed the central challenge at the start of the 20th century was "the question of national efficiency." As we start a new century we still face this challenge – and we have others as well.

Challenges

Legitimacy and Trust

One of the most significant challenges we face has to do with legitimacy: the extent to which we can trust the organizations we have created.

Every organization - regardless of whether it is a public company, an agency of government or a not-for-profit - requires the trust of people it serves to prosper. The difficulty is that too many us don't trust the institutions we have created. The challenge is serious: Warren Buffett has suggested what is at risk in the private sector is the loss of trust in "the most powerful wealth producing system in the world."[144] The companion risk in the public sector is the ability of government agencies and not-for-profit organizations to maintain the loyalty and support of people they serve.

The difficulty we have trusting organizations is usually a result of some combination of the following issues:

- Too many organizations focus on their own well being - organizational profits and operations rather than people and service.

- Too many organizations having trouble telling the truth.

"I guess I should warn you, if I turn out to be particularly clear, you've probably misunderstood what I said."
Alan Greenspan

William Lutz, an English professor at Rutgers University, coined the phrase 'double speak'[145] to describe the ways in which people and organizations use words to obscure the truth. Lutz identifies four forms of doublespeak:

1. euphemisms - words or phrases chosen to avoid reality. Businesses no longer lose money; they have "negative cash flow," "deficit enhancement," "net profit revenue deficiencies" or "negative contributions to profits;"
2. specialized jargon - companies don't fire people; they make "workforce adjustments," "census reductions," or institute programs of "negative employee retention."
3. 'gobbledygook'– words chosen to confuse or overwhelm an audience. Alan Greenspan, the widely respected and long-term chairman of the Federal

Reserve Board, has long been a master at this form of doublespeak. One of his memorable quotes was part of a speech to the Economic Club of New York.

4. inflated language – making the ordinary seem extraordinary. Used cars have now become "preowned" or "experienced cars."

It's hard to trust organizations when you can't understand what they are saying or can't be sure they mean what they say even when you do understand them.

Too many organizations do things that are just dumb, others that are foolish and still others that are egregious and, in some cases, criminal.

The Dumb: CBS Sports used to dub bird sounds to provide background at golf tournaments. Yulee Larner, a former President of the Virginia Ornithological Society, noticed the white-throated sparrow could be heard in the background at a tournament being played in Colorado – the difficulty was the bird isn't found in the region. Larner was delighted to hear the hermit thrush in the background at a tournament in Kentucky, but there was the same problem. It was silly and CBS stopped the practice: they now spread birdseed near microphones to attract birds.[146] Equally silly was the decision by CBS staff to retouch publicity pictures promoting Katie Couric. CBS wanted us to trust her as their new evening news anchor – and then let a staff member introduce her with photographs that been doctored to make her appear slimmer. It was dumb.[147]

The Foolish: Film critic David Manning of Connecticut's Ridgefield Press loved the movie *Hollow Man* and several other Sony movies. The difficulty was he didn't exist: Manning was the creation of two Sony executives who made him up and then wrote positive reviews.[148] Tribute MasterCard sends applications to potential customers offering a credit card with a $500 dollar limit. If the recipient accepts the card, and doesn't use it for a year, the fees would be $257. That's just wrong.[149]

The Egregious: The decision by Hewlett Packard executives to spy on members of the Board and senior executives is a particularly sad example of egregious behavior, especially given the company's rich history of serving as model of how companies should be run. What was called the 'H-P Way' was a symbol of excellence. The people involved in the spying foolishness disgraced themselves and betrayed the great traditions of one of the country's finest companies. The H-P case is a good example of Hartman's frustration with the law. What the people involved in the spying scandal did may or may not have been legal; it clearly was wrong.

The scandals and behavior associated with organizations that have achieved the notoriety of WorldCom, Enron and others has been much more serious. WorldCom's illegal behavior affected hundreds of thousands of people: among them the company's own employees who lost their pensions, stockholders who lost the value of their investments, vendors who lost business and had to lay off employees, people who worked for competitors who were terminated as those competitors tried to match WorldCom's profits and the thousands of people who worked for their vendors as well. The irony in these cases, and others like them, is senior executives who had previously justified their salaries by asserting they controlled their organizations and were personally responsible for their success suddenly began saying they knew little about the business or decisions made by the people who worked for them.

In other cases organizations have trouble doing what we expect them to do. Some crime laboratories have basic operating problems. These problems include missing files, contaminated evidence and results that have been misinterpreted.[150] Comair, the regional subsidiary of Delta Airlines cancelled 1,100 flights when it computer system crashed. The $14.6 billion dollar 'big dig' project in Boston had problems that led to the death of a newly married 38 year old woman and was described by Governor Mitt Romney as a "systemic failure, not an anomaly or a fluke."[151]

In each of these examples, the people and organizations involved either didn't use their judgment or were unable to do what was expected of them. In the examples of poor judgment, the people involved lacked understanding of the meaning of their actions or, more regrettably, understood what they were doing and went ahead anyway.

In the cases of system problems or cases in which people and organizations were unable to do what was expected of them, the issue usually involved an over reliance on scientific management.

> There's no right or wrong here, just business, and business is a shark swimming around and trying to eat every damned thing it comes across.
> Troon Mcallister, Scratch, 2004

Meaning and Work

A second challenge is the need for organizations and their leaders to understand work should have meaning.

The author Thomas Moore has pointed out one of the central dilemmas of our time is what he calls "the loss of soul."[152] In Moore's view, the soul has to do with genuineness and depth – what Hartman would have described as being fully who we are. The poet David Whyte talks about this loss of meaning when he talks about getting caught up in "busyness."[153] Peter Senge describes the same phenomenon well when he observes that: 'We often spend so much time coping with problems along our path that we forget why we are on that path in the first place. The result is that we only have a dim, or even inaccurate, view of what's really important to us.'[154]

One article in the Harvard Business Review began "Burned-out, bottlenecked and bored. That's the current lot of millions of mid-career employees."[155] In other more positive cases, employees in one client organization say things like "I understand what is expected of me at work.", "My job enables me to use my strengths.", "My supervisor communicates openly and honestly.", I am treated as a valuable member of my department." In these cases, the organization and its managers have been able to be clear about the meaning of the work and value of the people who do it.[156]

The point is that having to deal with the glut of information and respond to demands to do things more quickly often makes it harder for managers to remember what matters. In too many cases, organizations get so caught up in either managing the systems they have created or trying to achieve short-term financial results that the work they actually do loses its meaning.

For most of us work, is only a part of our lives. It may, and should be, an important part, but it is still only one aspect of who we are. When we are not at work, some of us volunteer to read stories in our children's kindergarten, others write poetry, others sing in church choirs and still others referee high school sports events.[157] The meaning of what we do with our lives matters to us and organizations suffer when they lose sight of the fact that we want work to have the same meaning as activities we care about in other parts of our lives. The fact is, as the demographic forecaster Bruce Clarke eloquently puts it, "people like work; it's jobs they can't stand."[158]

Change

A third organizational challenge is the need to deal effectively with change. We have always had change, but the point now is the process of change is different than what it was for previous generations.

Specifically the changes organizations experience are different now because they are:

- Faster - Changes that used to occur over centuries and lifetimes now occur within lifetimes, decades and sometimes just years. Europe went through the industrial period in 200 years, the United States in a 100 and Japan in approximately 50.
  Changes in air transportation are a good example of changes that have occurred over a single lifetime. My

grandfather was born in 1900, which meant he was 3 years old when Wilbur and Orville Wright made their first plane flight, he was 27 when Charles Lindberg flew from Long Island to Paris, 46 when Trans World Airlines made the first commercial intercontinental flight from New York-to-Paris service; and 69 when astronaut Neil Armstrong took 'one small step for man and one giant leap for mankind' on the moon July 20, 1969. In the space of my grandfather's lifetime we went from learning to fly to landing on the moon.

- Pervasive - Change now affects every area of our personal and organizational lives simultaneously. Job expectations have changed, the emergence of televangelists and mega churches has changed how many of us worship; where we shop has changed as well: Wal-Mart is now the nation's largest grocery store, Costco is the largest seller of wines, General Motors is one of the nation's largest banks and UPS is major computer service company.

- Constant - People in earlier generations organized their lives around the idea of stability and understood changes as interruptions in an otherwise stable world. There might be change, but after whatever changes occurred things would 'return to normal.' Now, the reverse is true: change is the constant and stability is the exception. As numerous clients have pointed out: "It's always something."

> Change is the constant;
> stability is the exception.

These changes in change itself mean people and organizations that want stability will invariably – and always - be disappointed.

The changes in the nature of change are one of the clear reasons we have to think about how we manage differently; when the world changes constantly, there can never be a stable 'one best way.'

Technology

Organizations in every field have to deal with the impact of emerging technologies. The challenge is real, because all emerging technologies share the following four characteristics.

- First, they become (in some combination) smaller, faster and cheaper. This is especially true of technologies that have their roots in computer chips and communications systems. The original ENIAC (Electrical Numerical Integrator And Calculator) computer was patented on June 26, 1947. It contained 17,468 vacuum tubes, along with 70,000 resistors, 10,000 capacitors, 1,500 relays, 6,000 manual switches and 5 million soldered joints. It covered 1,800 square feet of floor space, weighed 30 tons and consumed 160 kilowatts of electrical power.[159]

- By contrast, the Apple Ipod weighs 5.6 ounces, has a 60-gigabyte hard disk drive that holds thousand songs and serves as a backup disk drive. Adidas (and others) now make sneakers that include computer sensors to adjust the softness of the midsole to respond instantaneously to running conditions.[160] Nike and Apple have now developed a running shoe that transmits data to an Ipod. In each case the capacity of new technologies exceeds those of the ENIAC by geometric orders of magnitude.

- Second, emerging technologies provide us with, as the philosopher Heinz Pagels observed, "a new angle on reality."[161]

- Linda Dillman's ability to go through thousands of bits of Wal-Mart data to determine what people would buy after a hurricane is one example of how our perceptions of reality change because of the capabilities of new technologies. Tools we now take for granted – such as simple Excel spreadsheets – enable us to manage more data and analyze it from different perspectives than Frederick Taylor and his colleagues could ever have imagined. High powered telescopes enable us to explore the universe and magnetic resonance imaging (MRI) technology lets us explore minute changes in brainwaves in the human mind.[162]

- Third, new technologies raise questions about the relationship between ourselves and the machines we have created.

- In the early 1900s, the primary benefit of most new technologies was their contribution to enhancing physical capabilities: steam shovels, railroads and machinery enabled us to physically do more and do it faster.

- Now technological innovation is different. Ray Kurzweil has written about 'sentient machines' – machines that have feelings - and his ideas have touched off debates about what may or may not be the limits of computers and emerging technologies.[163] Kurzweil writes that "by 2009 computers will be embedded in our clothes. By 2019 they will be embedded in our bodies. By 2099, human and machine intelligence will have merged."[164] Kurzweil's forecasts may be conservative: computers are already embedded in clothing materials to control temperature. Similarly, cardiac pacemakers are already embedded in our bodies to control otherwise defective hearts.

- In this same vein, Bill Joy, one of the original developers of Sun Microsystems, has suggested the machines we are creating will be capable of acting independently. Joy has gone further and suggested machines may not need us, because we are too emotional and inefficient.[165]

- While Joy's suggestions have a certain dramatic flair, there are already machines that act as he describes. Clothes dryers determine when clothes are dry and turn themselves off. Rain-sensing windshield wipers are now standard in many luxury model cars.[166] Selfdefrosting refrigerators and automobile braking systems are other everyday examples now so common we take them for granted. Sonar systems now help fisherman track fish. These systems are a good example of Pagel's observation about how technologies change our angle on reality. In this case these technologies prompted writer Joshua Davis to question at what point fishing became too easy.[167]

- Finally, developments in biotechnology raise questions about the meaning of life itself.

- We have had the capability to replace physical body parts such as knees, hips and hearts for some time. Now, we are learning how to manipulate molecular and genetic structures to alter and design or redesign human life itself. Mood altering drugs that bring relief to people suffering from depression are one example of this ability to reshape our behavior and to some extent alter who we are.

- Given developments in biotechnology, we are going to have to go beyond extrinsic thinking about how to manage new technologies and think intrinsically about what they mean as well.

Complexity

Simply put, every area of our lives is increasingly complex – and in many cases too complex.

- Products. The instructions to put in a basic child's safety car seat in the back seat a car take 39 pages;
- Legislative process. The number of bills introduced in the Arkansas legislature increased by 41% between 1997 and 2003.[168]
- Organizations. The media analyst and writer, Ken Auletta, observed that between 1977 and 1987, the number of stories on the NBC evening news dropped from 2,496 to 1,564, while the cost of each story went from $12,400 to $63,000. Of the total number of reporters, the top 10 accounted for over 85% of the stories that aired. There were fewer stories featuring fewer people, while the costs for people and producing the stories went up. The executives responsible initially defended how they ran the news division, because they had always done it that way.[169]

The point is clear: our organizations are too complex; there is too much paper and too many steps in the processes we use to accomplish what we need to do.

Meetings are a wonderful example. Managers complain about too many meetings or to say it more carefully, they complain not that there are too many meetings but that we have the same meeting over and over again. According to one study too many meetings actually make us 'grumpy.'[170] In a study printed in *Group Dynamics*, two social science researchers found that – in language that reflects the earlier discussion about meaning and work - meetings left employees feeling stressed, exhausted and burned out.

This complexity is the inevitable result of a preoccupation with an approach to management that emphasizes refining 'the system' and too little attention to determining whether what we are doing makes sense or needs to be done at all.

Robert Hartman's observation was that: "When rules, procedures, regulations and systems prevail over people, when there is pressure to meet the quotas, and when the quotas are always being raised there will always be problems." [171] Hartman was right when he said it forty years ago and his observation is even more important today

Approaches

Over the last several decades, we have tried to deal with these challenges and the approaches we have taken have tended to fall into one or more of three broad categories.

More and Better Scientific Management

The 'more and better' approach has been based on applying updated versions of Frederick Taylor's original ideas. These have included 'quality,' 'lean', kaizen, Six Sigma and numerous other contemporary versions of Taylor's scientific management. The result is a continuing introduction of new 'programs of the week' that lead to confusion among managers and cynicism among workers who find it hard to overcome the belief that management's interest in this 'program of the week' will be replaced by the next new idea a week, month or year later.

The problem is whichever one of these 'more is better' approaches is chosen, it is usually implemented in a vacuum: the focus is on the program (the extrinsic) rather than a balanced approach based on people (the intrinsic) and systems (the systemic). Very few of us want to work for the sake of 'hitting a number' – most of us will do what needs to be done when we understand why it matters.

Scientific management efforts that focus on efficiency will inevitably fall short of what they can achieve when managers remember that the personal, practical and systemic need to be in balance.

Structural Approaches

One of the great scientific insights ideas of the early 1900s was that structure mattered. Now as we start a new century, it is clear relationships matter as much as or more than structure.

The structural approach has limitations because it turns our attention inward toward the organization and how it works in the present rather than outward toward the people it serves and the future. Example: a frequent debate in organizations is whether they should centralize or decentralize decision-making. From Taylor's perspective the question centers on the system: which approach will help us achieve the one best way. From Hartman's perspective the question centers on asking which approach will best serve people.

> Good people can overcome weaknesses in structure but, the reverse isn't true.

Structure is important, but a preoccupation with it overlooks the reality that in every organization people accomplish work because of personal relationships – not because of formal structures. These may be the relationships they have developed with colleagues in their own departments, people in other departments or people they work with in other organizations, but the point is that it is the relationships rather than the structure that matters. In speeches over 20 years, when I have asked people if they look at the organization chart to determine who they should talk to solve a problem the reaction is usually giggles or outright laughter – people don't look at the organization chart; they ask their friends and colleagues they trust to identify people who can help them get done what they need to do.

Personal Approaches – People and Politics

Other organizations have emphasized the intrinsic. These approaches usually stress personal relationships, collaboration, team building and the need for people to work together.

The personal approach is apparent in conversations when managers talk about the organization as a family.

- Families are bound by blood; organizations are bound by a common purpose and the ability of people to contribute to achieving that purpose.

- You are in a family throughout your life; you are part of an organization as long as the relationship is mutually beneficial.

- In most families regardless of your behavior, you are still a part of the family; organizations have standards and people who don't meet them leave voluntarily or are asked to leave.

The personal approach is important, but there are problems when organizations emphasize it at the expense of the practical or systemic.

Hartman recognized when organizations overemphasize people and the intrinsic, they get in every bit as much trouble as when they overemphasize the extrinsic and scientific management – it was the reason he was so insistent on balance.

Economics: Money, Finance and Motivation

The economic approach is based on the idea money is a key motivator and organizations can create a clear relationship between what we want people to do and how they are paid. These two ideas were a central part of Taylor's use of money to motivate 'his men.'

The approach works well in some cases but not so well in others. The problem has been especially difficult in determining how to compensate senior executives. Corporate boards have tried various approaches and to date none has been satisfactory. The point is clear: structural and economic approaches won't work, because anyone who wants to will always find a way to beat the system. We can never design a system that 'can't be beat' so we have to find other ways to encourage people to behave sensibly.

Organizing for Good

Organizing for good provides a more useful framework for thinking about organizations and management. The approach differs from scientific management, because it values systems and practical elements of an organization to the extent they support people. The difference is apparent in the schematics Hartman used to describe organizing for good.

A graphic representation of an organization run according to Taylor's scientific management looks like this:

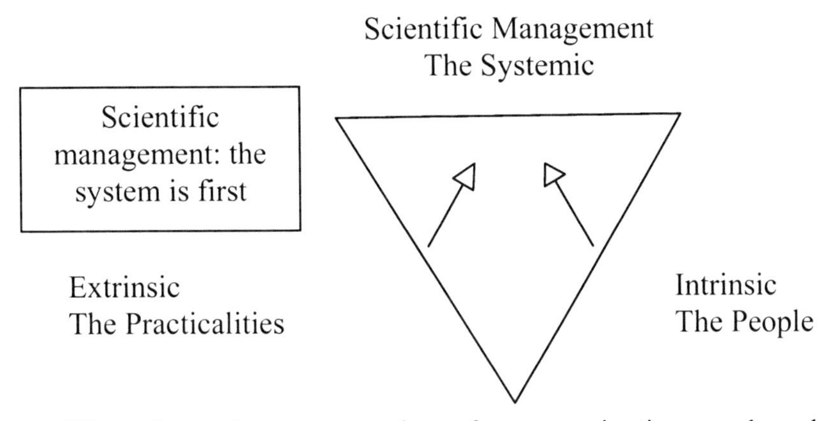

The schematic representation of an organization run based on the idea of organizing for good looks like this:

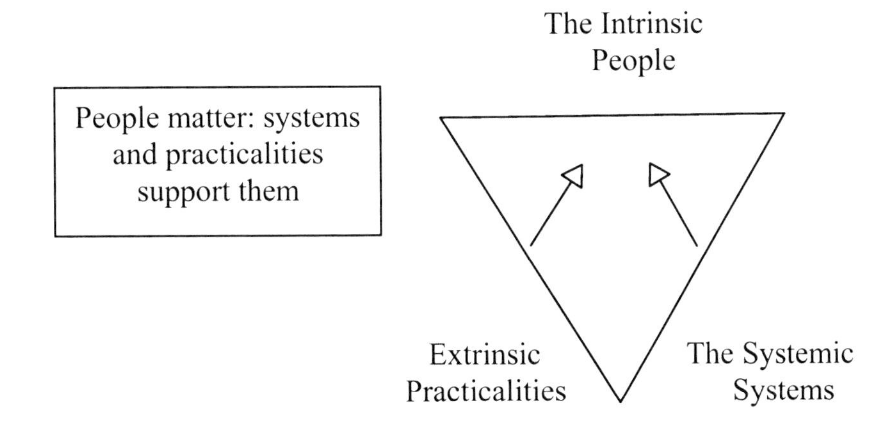

Managing the Intrinsic

Managing the intrinsic means the organization focuses on the people it serves and affects. Managing the intrinsic means organizations are committed to hiring the best candidates and then placing people in positions where they can be effective and develop their capabilities.

The key point in managing the intrinsic side of an organization is to remember that what they accomplish is, as my friend Peter Fraser observes, because of people not in spite of them.

Choose People Well

The first thing effective organizations do is pay attention to who they hire.

In these organizations, managers understand choosing who they hire is one of their most important responsibilities rather than a distraction that takes time away from their real work.

In his books Good to Great and Built to Last, Jim Collins emphasizes the importance of people. Collins' conclusions were based on an analysis of hundreds of organizations.[172] Hartman's work provides the framework for Collins's analysis. Collins reached his conclusions based on his analysis; several decades earlier Hartman reached the same conclusions by thinking about what it meant to organize for good.

In contrast to Taylor's view that his men should "do what they were told" Hartman's approach and Collins's research highlight the importance of judgment and how people make decisions.

In simple terms, choosing people well means managers hire carefully because they know it improves the quality of the work force and the effectiveness of the organization.

Right People Right Work

The second intrinsic consideration is placing people in positions that are consistent with how they make decisions.

Some jobs require discipline and the ability to follow directions; financial management, bookkeeping and the willingness to perform rote tasks on an ongoing basis are examples. Others, such as corporate planning functions require the systemic capacity to see patterns. Still others, such as marketing and selling, are best filled by people with a strong sense of self worth.

Research using the Hartman Value Profile clarifies the importance of judgment. Successful middle managers have a stronger systemic orientation and are generally balanced across the three dimensions. Effective senior executives, those who are respected and effective rather than incompetent or self-centered, are usually balanced and have strong intrinsic capacities. They are able to energize people and build commitment to what needs to be done. They have the technical capabilities Kronman and others said were important and those technical capabilities support their ability to work with people. The important point is technical skills by themselves are useful in middle management and necessary but not adequate to be effective as a senior manager. Senior managers need to be balanced. Those who are good with people but lack practical skills (the extrinsic) or the capacity to see patterns and plan (the systemic) are likely to be ineffective.

Developing Recognizing and Rewarding Judgment

Developing and rewarding judgment means we have to be honest with people, let them know where they stand and reward them for performance.

Weak performance review systems get organizations into trouble for several reasons. First, they allow weaker managers to avoid dealing honestly with their employees. The phenomenon is an example of systemic and intrinsic weakness in the organization. Weak managers tend to be unclear about how what they do relates to the overall strategy of the organization – a systemic weakness - and therefore are unable to set standards for their employees, because they don't know what is expected of them or what should be expected of their employees.

Every performance review should cover three areas: what the employee does well, what he/she do adequately and what he/she need to improve. By definition we can't be good at everything, because it would assume, in Hartman's terms, that we have reached our full potential and become fully who we ought to be. Not straightforwardly telling an employee what they need to improve denies the employee the opportunity to grow. It's unfair, dishonest and wrong.

The first part of developing and rewarding people's performance means organizations care and respect their employees enough to tell them the truth. It also means they have clear written standards for what needs to be done (the systemic) and consistent expectations for how people will be evaluated (the extrinsic.) When organizations are committed to organizing for good, performance reviews, like the hiring process, become an important management responsibility. This approach reflects Hartman's belief in the importance of the intrinsic as well as Herzberg's insights about what actually motivates employees. Recognizing and rewarding performance provides each of us the opportunity to be acknowledged for what we have accomplished and gain a better understanding of how we can improve.

The second part has to do with investing in staff development. We used to be able to think of our lives as linear experiences: we would go to school, grow up, get married, work and then retire. Because this linear world was generally stable, we could apply what we learned in our youth throughout our careers.

Now, because of the challenges discussed earlier, each of us has to continue to learn throughout our lives. Effective organizations invest in the training and development of Boards, their executives, managers and staff, because it improves the organizations competence and the ability of its employees to grow, learn and become increasingly effective. Money spent on training is an investment – not a cost because it improves the staff's judgment and ability to do work well.

Effective organizations invest in developing employee capabilities and then recognize and reward performance, because it provides the most direct way for both the organization and the individual to become what they ought to be.

A Note on People and Teams

> "Under the right conditions groups are smarter than the smartest person in them."
> James Surweicki
> Wired Magazine
> June 2006, page 87

Teams and collaboration are increasingly important; learning to use them well means thinking differently about how we organize them.

A team is a group of people with a common purpose and objectives they need to accomplish together. A well-structured team will include three types of people: a) people doing the work; b) people affected by the work being done; and c) others who have insights, experience or understandings that can contribute to the work of the group.

Thinking about teams differently means, first, teams will always have attributes that are distinct and different from the attributes of any of its individual members. The Miami Heat basketball team, for example, has a character and personality that is distinct from individual players such as Shaquille O'Neal or Dwayne Wade. Second, thinking differently about teams means understanding what 'consensus' means. We tend to think consensus means we have discussed an issue and everyone agrees. It doesn't. General Electric has a better definition recognizes the importance of diversity and the need for organizational discipline. In General Electric's view:

> Consensus does not mean that everyone agrees. It does mean that everyone agrees to implement and actively support the decision, because they believe their reservations and concerns were heard and considered and that the decision is the best under the circumstances.

Third, thinking about teams differently means we have to think about diversity differently. Diversity is important because it ensures perspectives that might not otherwise be considered are part of the discussion. Groups that are too much alike find it hard to learn because each member brings less new information to the table. Homogeneous groups are good at doing what they do well but are less able to investigate alternatives or conceive of a future different from the present.

Diverse teams include people who have a wide range of experiences and perspectives. In practical terms, diverse teams include people drawn from different operating units – i.e. manufacturing, sales and finance - depending on the nature of the work to be done. Finally, in Hartman terms, it includes people who are animated by intrinsic, extrinsic and systemic considerations.

There are examples of situations in which teams have been especially effective. At Pixar films, the producers of movie hits such as Toy Story, Monsters and Cars, people stay together through successive projects. Unlike traditional Hollywood practices in which groups working on projects are assembled for a single project and then move on other work, Pixar believes there is a value in continuity. The Allen Edmonds Shoe Company expanded facilities in the United States in the belief that if people could work in teams rather than independently and the company invested in the technology to support them, the company would be more successful than if they outsourced the work.[173]

The intrinsic is an essential component of organizing for good, but effective organizations are clear about extrinsic and systemic requirements to design teams well.

Extrinsic

Extrinsic considerations are important, because they provide the bridge between the abstract world of planning and ideas and the practical ability to do what needs to be done to serve people. Organizing for good means organizations master four issues: simplicity, accountability and discipline, operating excellence and innovation.

Simplicity

Organizing for good requires simplicity.

The principle goes back as far as Aristotle who made the point that 'nature operates in the shortest way possible.' William of Occam, a 14th century Franciscan Friar wrote 'when you have two competing theories, which make exactly the same predictions, the one that is simpler is the better."[174] Scientists talk about an elegant theory as a theory that embraces all of the known facts without extraneous components or considerations.

> "Most employees and teammates – even the well intentioned – make things far too complicated."
>
> Bill Jensen
> Simplicity, 2001

In the early part of the last century, Henry Ford exemplified simplicity: he kept the same Model T design for 15 million Model Ts from 1908 until 1927.[175] In this century, Fred Brooks, the manager of IBM's System/360 and OS/360 software efforts, wrote in his 1975 book The Mythical Man-Month that 'adding people to a late software project makes it later:"[176] rather than helping accelerate progress, additional people added complexity and slowed the work down.

Abraham Lincoln was once asked how long a man's legs should be, he responded by saying "long enough to reach the ground." The point is clear: simplicity is an essential component of achieving excellence and organizing for good.

Complexity is a problem for three reasons.

First, things that are complex are hard to understand. Second, products and processes that are complex are more likely to break down. Third, products and processes that are complex are more expensive than those that are simple.

This means we need to simplify people, paper and processes.

- People – organizations need to have the correct number of people to do the work that needs to be done. People create complexity. When organizations have too few people, they burn out and do poor work. When organizations have too many, managers and staff create processes, paper and unnecessary work.

- Paper – much of the paper work in most organizations is either duplicative or unnecessary. Effective organizations reduce paper.

- Processes – simple processes reduce complexity and costs and make it easier for people to do what needs to be done and do it well.

Accountability and Discipline

Organizing for good means the organization is disciplined and people associated with it are accountable for what they do.

These qualities have been hard to achieve because we misunderstand what discipline means. Most of us tend to view discipline as a constraint on freedom rather than the quality that enables us to be free. When organizations are disciplined and effective, people are free to do what needs to be done. Conversely, when organizations lack discipline, people spend time on office politics, cajoling the reluctant, writing unnecessary memos and emails, copying their boss's bosses and numerous others on memos and emails, debating what needs to be done and endlessly jockeying for position.

Being disciplined means managers and employees have straightforward discussions abut what needs to be done. In these organizations, people say what they mean and mean what they say. It also means they do what they say they will do. In these organizations, people complete assignments on time, return telephone calls and complete responsibilities such as personnel evaluations effectively and on time.

There is a striking difference between the behavior and language in organizations that are disciplined and those that are not.

Organizational Language and Action

Disciplined	Undisciplined
The Intrinsic – People	
Clear performance standards and job descriptions	Vague expectations – uneven or non-existent evaluations
The Extrinsic – Culture	
Clear operating systems	Confusion about 'how we do things' – different operating procedures in individual units
Meetings with clear agendas based on strategic priorities	Long, wandering meetings with much aimless discussion to understand issues that may or may not matter
The Extrinsic - Vision	
Strategic focus – limited number of priorities	Operating short term focus – constantly changing priorities - long lists of priorities and 'things to do'
Clear goals and objectives	Changing goals and objectives – numerous 'crises' and 'programs of the week'

Similarly, there are differences in language in effective and ineffective organizations. The language in undisciplined organizations includes phrases such as 'we're working on it,' the (chose one) committee/task force/process team is working on it', 'I'm not sure,' 'They're dealing with that', 'I'll find out and get back to you', or 'They (whoever they are) won't cooperate. The language is usually process oriented and filled with vague phrases and responses. In disciplined organizations by contrast, people talk about what has been accomplished and dates by which work either has or will be done. People in these organizations are clear about who is responsible and what they will do.

When organizations are undisciplined, there is a lack of clarity. It is difficult for people to know what is expected of them, hard for managers and staff to evaluate each other and, not surprisingly, difficult to hold people responsible when things go wrong or reward them when things go well.

Operating Excellence

Effective organizations are committed to operating excellence.

Taylor was correct about the benefits of systems. He was wrong when he put systems ahead of people. Similarly, today's managers are wrong when they think of achieving operational excellence as an end in itself rather than as being important, because it enables them to serve people well.

When properly understood strong, and well-understood operating systems make it easier for people to communicate, because there is a shared vocabulary and common understanding of what words mean. These systems make it easier to clarify expectations and everyone who is part of them to understand what is expected of them.

The difficulty many organizations have when they try to implement a consistent system operating is the systems are seen as another ploy to increase profits or as an end in themselves rather than a way to help employees become more effective and enable the organization to serve people well.

Innovation

Because change is constant, innovation is an essential part of organizing for good.

Peter Drucker identified seven sources of opportunities for innovation:

1. The Unexpected - An unexpected success, failure or outside event can be a symptom of a unique opportunity.
2. The Incongruity - A discrepancy between reality and what everyone assumes it to be, or between what is and what ought to be, can create an innovative opportunity.
3. Innovation based on process need - When a weak link is evident in a particular process, but people work around it instead of doing something about it, an opportunity is present to the person or company willing to supply the "missing link".
4. Changes in industry or market structure - The opportunity for an innovative product, service or business approach occurs when the underlying foundation of the industry or market shifts.
5. Demographics - Changes in the population's size, age structure, composition, employment, level of education and income can create innovative opportunities.
6. Changes in perception, mood and meaning - Innovative opportunities can develop when a society's general assumptions, attitudes and beliefs change.
7. New Knowledge - Advances in scientific and nonscientific knowledge can create new products and new markets.

Innovation is essential because there will always be a new idea or better way. Successful organizations promote and encourage innovation.

Values

Values are most usefully thought of as characteristics that shape our behavior, rather than as attributes we possess. A United States Army pamphlet – *Values: The Bedrock of Our Profession*: states "Values are what we, as a profession, judge to be right. They

> "We will not be measured by our aspirations. We will be measured buy our actions."
>
> Lee Scott, Chairman WalMart
> Marc Gunther,
> The Green Machine,
> Fortune Magazine

are more than words - they are the moral ethical and professional attributes of character."[177]

Organizational values are essential, because they provide the framework and guidance for how managers and staff are expected to make decisions. When they are well understood, people throughout an organization know what is expected of them. In Hartman's terms it is the extrinsic and practical abilities to act on what we believe enables individuals and organizations to become fully who they ought to be.

Scientific management is useful because the approach helps us figure out how to do something: it is not useful in helping us determine whether what we are doing is the right thing to do. The difficulty comes when organizations fail to act on what they say they believe. One company stated in their Principles of Human Rights they would "treat others as we would like to be treated" and "work with customers and prospects openly, honestly and sincerely." The company was Enron and the obvious problem was while they had clear statements of principle (the systemic), they failed to act on them (the extrinsic) and, as a result, people got hurt. Enron did well at scientific management; they ran the business and met the numbers. They failed miserably at organizing for good because the leadership was corrupt. When people and organizations become preoccupied with the systemic or the extrinsic, they invariably get into trouble because becoming preoccupied with efficiency obscures the questions of whether what we are doing is appropriate.

The United States Coast Guard is good example of an organization having clear values and the ability to act on them. Interestingly, the Coast Guard has never had a clear consistent mission. Over the course of its history, it collected taxes from smugglers, chased pirates, rescued people at sea, and worked on oil cleanup projects. Wil Milam, one of the Coast Guard's rescue swimmers, says the point is to take care of people and the mission will take care of itself. This sense of values is reflected in stories of Coast Guard officers ignoring superiors to make decisions about what they thought was right for people. Clear Coast Guard values include the ability to improvise, a commitment to decentralization and a reliance on accountability, because as one officer says the Coast Guard is so small "There's no place to hide," so people make decisions and take risks.[178]

Another example: Jeffrey Immelt, the Chairman of General Electric has talked about four qualities he believes will keep General Electric successful; one of them is virtue. Immelt argues to be a great company you have to be a good company and says "good leaders give back. The era we live in belongs to people who believe in themselves but are focused on the needs of others." Immelt makes it clear that operational excellence and productivity are still important, but it is equally clear he has moved beyond scientific management. At the same time, he is clear that "if this wasn't good for business, we probably wouldn't do it."[179] From this perspective, Immelt has embodied Harman's belief in the importance of the intrinsic and the need to balance the intrinsic with the practical and the systemic.

Vision

A vision of the future is important, because it provides a framework for decisions, clarity about what the organization believes matters and, if sufficiently compelling, engages people who will do the work in the pursuit of the vision.

> If you don't care where you're going, you're not lost.

Some organizations use vision statements as descriptions of their desired future; others use them to clarify what matters to them. However they are used, vision statements clarify how the organization will make decisions. They matter, especially during periods of change, because they help people and organizations clarify what matters. The Tattered Cover bookstore in Denver has a clear vision. According to the owner Joyce Meskis "it's all about the books."[180] That vision may not meet a purist's standard for what a mission statement ought to be, but it provides the basis for decisions to she made to give 1% of its pre-tax profits to not-for-profit community organizations, sponsor author presentations, hire knowledgeable staff, defend privacy rights in cases that have gone to the Supreme Court and sponsor events such as "Banned Book Week," which as the stores web site says 'reminds Americans not to take reading, a precious democratic freedom, for granted.'[181] Mike Eskew, the Chairman of UPS, says the company's vision is 'to enable commerce.' UPS repairs Toshiba laptops, manages warehouses with spare parts for Bentley automobiles and supply stores for Nike.[182]

Debates about distinctions between an organization's mission, values and vision will continue; what matters is that however it's constructed or used it has meaning for people in the organization.

Money and Finance

Brandeis's original argument drew national and worldwide attention to Taylor's work and, more specifically, to issues related to costs. Over time, this attention to costs and the efficient use of capital has become a central, if not the central, focus of organizational executives. The difficulty is that we have lost balance and an understanding of the meaning of money, and more specifically, net income. Increasing net income and cash flow has become an end in itself rather than a means of understanding how we can achieve excellence.

Net income tells us three things about an organization:

1. How well it understands the people it serves. If an organization understands the people it serves and produces products or services they need, net income goes up – when it doesn't net income goes down. Example. When Ford Motor produced the Edsel and

few people bought it Ford lost money. (Ford sold 110,000 cars over a 3 year period; by comparison the Chevrolet Impala sold [number]. Conversely, shortly after Steven Jobs introduced the Apple Ipod On October 23, 2001 sales began to grow rapidly. No amount of efficiency can overcome the problems that come from making something nobody wants.

2. How simple the systems are. When systems are simple and make it easier for people to do their jobs, net income goes up. When systems are complex they become increasingly expensive and net income goes down. Hartman's point was that a thing is good to the extent that is what it ought to be. The application for organizations is that their systems should be no more complex than necessary. This point reinforces Taylor's central point about the need to reduce variation to improve quality.
   The difficulty has been that organizations have focused on the 'program of the week' (the extrinsic aspect of variation) through efforts such as 'quality', 'reengineering', process management or any one of a number of others rather than focusing on the value of simplicity and the idea of striving for excellence.

3. How well people get along and how well they are placed in positions consistent with what Robert Hartman called value tendencies. First, when people get along and help each other, quality goes up and costs go down. This is another example of the idea that when people don't get along, costs go up: they write more memos; hold more meetings to clarify what needs to be done and hire more staff, because they don't trust their colleagues. When they get along, they talk to each other about what needs to be done; have fewer meeting because they understand each other and need fewer

> people, because they go out of their way to help each other adjust to changes in what they need to do. Second, when people are doing work that is consistent with their value tendencies, they are more effective than when they are doing work that asks them to change who they are. Some people are disciplined; others value creativity. Some are able to deal with difficult people; others aren't. This doesn't, as Hartman consistently pointed out, make them good or bad; it makes them different. When people do work and are in positions consistent with their value tendencies, they are invariably more effective than when they aren't.

The preoccupation with money as an end in itself rather than a way to gain insight into ways we can improve our effectiveness always leads to trouble. When organizational leaders focus on financial manipulations rather than the business itself sooner or later they get into trouble – and sometimes into court. The litany of scandals over the last decade has in large part resulted from this confusion and the meaning of money.

It's as simple as understanding that focusing on money as an end itself leads to trouble. Serving people well and caring about what you do leads to success.

Chapter 5

Summary

Great transformations have two common attributes.

First, they change institutions and how people work. Two good examples of how the process works are in agriculture and retailing.

In the middle 1800s, farmers began changing how they farmed. The 1862 Morrill Act [183] directed the land-grant colleges it created to do agricultural research and the results encouraged farmers to use scientifically-based information to make decisions in much the same way Taylor would introduce scientific management to manufacturers decades later. Shortly after the turn of century farming changed again: tractors and machinery began to do what men and animals had done previously. In the latter half of the 20th century farmers adjusted again: this time to globalization, the emergence of an information society and the development of computers. Tractors and combines now process information on crops and global financial markets as routinely as draft animals once ploughed the fields. This ability of farmers to adjust, adopt new technologies and improve their productivity has been one of the extraordinary achievements of the last 200 years.

Retailers have demonstrated this same ability to adapt to a changing environment. In the 1800s, as the country expanded, a young railroad clerk began to sell goods to people in small towns along the railroad line. Richard Sears took advantage of early communications technology - the telegraph - and transportation technology – the railroads - to bring products to people in small towns. Retailers adapted the growth of the cities with downtown department stores, the emergence of the suburbs with malls and more recently to the internet with web sites enabling people to shop from anywhere they choose.

The second significant characteristic of great transformations is they encourage the development of entirely new industries, institutions and ways of doing things.

The small family farm has given way to the agricultural conglomerate and the neighborhood grocery store that sold us food has given way to the supermarket that bas a bank, a post office and sells us tickets to symphonies and sports events, as well as groceries. The emergence of the automotive and clothing industries in the early 1900s, and more recently, the computer and information industries are examples of entirely new industries that have developed since 1911. Companies such as eBay and Amazon.com, not to mention even newer companies such as Myspace.com and Youtube.com are examples of these new institutions.

This process of transformation doesn't mean we throw out all we have learned; and, more specifically, it doesn't mean we abandon scientific management. It does mean we need to manage differently and, more importantly, think about what it means to achieve excellence and organize for good.

The following seven points, become the basis for how we need to think about management – and how we need to manage.

1. <u>People Matter: Systems Can Be Changed</u>

Organizing for good means we need to understand systems have value to the extent they benefit people: they have little value when they become ends in themselves.

When we organize for good, the key question is: 'What does what I am doing mean for people?" rather than "How can I make the system more efficient."

Some managers and companies already think this way. Their work has been described under labels such as 'mass customization,' 'customer service' or 'exceeding expectations' - but whatever the label, the focus is on putting people first. EBay is the 21st century electronic version of the town square; people come together through the Internet rather than walking to the town square. EBay has 114,000,000 registered worldwide users who buy, sell and trade products in 50,000 categories containing 2,9000,000 items trading at the rate of 1,020 each second.[184] Clothing companies such as Levi Strauss and Brooks Brothers use communications and information technologies to individually fit blue jeans and suits. Benefit plans have also changed: a growing number of companies now have some form of 'cafeteria benefit plans' for their employees. Traditional approaches based on a limited number of fixed and well-defined benefits are giving way to 'cafeteria plans' that provide a wider range of choices to respond to the needs of an increasingly diverse work force. In medicine, pharmaceutical researchers are focused on the development of 'designer drugs.' These hold the promise of replacing drugs that provide general relief to masses of people with drugs individually tailored to each person's individual condition and genetic makeup.

2. Effectiveness Matters More Than Efficiency

Achieving excellence means focusing on effectiveness rather than efficiency.

Efficiency limits our thinking to how well a system accomplishes what it is intended to do; effectiveness encourages us to think about how well systems meet the needs of people they are intended to serve.

In 2006, Dell Computer had to deal with customer technical

support issues that highlight the difference. Dell has always focused on speed and in customer support, this focus translated into metrics that measured how many calls technical support people could handle. The focus was on the system and the number of calls Dell technical people handled, rather than customers and how well their questions were answered. Not surprisingly, efficiency went up and customer satisfaction went down. As Michael Dell belatedly observed: "When you handle the call faster, you solve 90% of the problem, instead of 100%." Now Dell focuses on how well they solve the customer's problem rather than the number of calls the technical person handles. The result is better customer service and more effective systems. There were 2 million fewer customer service calls because Dell customers got their questions answered on the first call rather than having to call back – the system had become more effective - and more efficient.[185]

Focusing on effectiveness will always lead to greater efficiency.

3. Balance is Essential: There is no one best way

> There never has and never will be one best way.

Russell Ackoff, the organizational theorist and Anheuser Busch Professor Emeritus of management science at the Wharton School, has the clearest explanation for why there never has - and never will be - one best way. Ackoff's point is simple: you can a) optimize the system or b) optimize the subsystem; but c) optimizing one means that by definition you can not optimize the other.

The 'best way' to do work in a single unit will never be the best way for another unit or the organization as a whole. Designing an effective system means managers have to make judgments about how to balance the competing and legitimate needs of the overall system and its components: you can't optimize both.

In addition to the system problem Ackoff describes, managers will never be able to develop one durable best way, because they have to adjust to change. The reality, as one client has said is 'that it's always something.'

Thinking about balance encourages managers to think about how to balance the needs of their own department with the needs of other departments and the organization as a whole. It also encourages them to think about people - how what they do affects customers, colleagues, shareholders, suppliers or anyone else their actions may touch. It turns their attention to people and effectiveness rather than efficiency and systems.

4. Encourage People to Develop and Use Their Judgment

> You can't automate judgment.
> Ivan Wellborn, ATO Findley

Taylor was trying to eliminate judgment; in 2006 encouraging employees to use their judgment is essential.

Effective leaders understand Peter Fraser's observation that companies "are successful because of people, not in spite of them.' People who care about their work and understand what they are doing and why it matters will always outperform people who are 'going through the motions.' The discipline of Taylor's systems and his desire to eliminate workers using their judgment is an especially good example of an idea that may have worked well in the past but won't work now or in the future. Herzberg's work over 50 years and the practicalities every managers grapple with today make it clear most employees want to be engaged with their work and proud of what they do.

Thinking differently is an essential first step; but, as Robert Hartman would have pointed out, thinking differently (the systemic) is not enough – we have to act differently and this means changing how we manage.

In addition to the points in the discussions of people and organizations, there are additional steps we can take to manage more effectively. These are described below as transitions from what we do now to what we can do to be more effective in the future.

5. Manage By Value First; Rules Second

Organizing for good means understanding values matter more than rules.

In almost every case of executive malfeasance, the argument for the defense has been the same: what the executive or the company did didn't break the law. This was the point Robert Hartman reached early in his career; the law could tell you what was legal or not legal but not was right or wrong. The defendants and their lawyers may be right; but the standard is too low.

There will probably always be executives who focus on rules rather than values. Some politicians will choose to comply with the letter, rather than the spirit, of campaign finance law; some business leaders will enrich themselves at the expense of others; some academics will skirt the edges of intellectual integrity. Some people will always decide they can beat the system.

The positive side of recent personal and corporate scandals has been a growing understanding of the importance of values. Business schools have begun to develop courses on ethics to address the problem Warren Bennis and James O' Toole described. At the Harvard Business School, ethics courses that were optional in the 1980s have now become mandatory.[186] Legislative and regulatory requirements may be helpful, but organizing for good means we need to understand that complying with rules is the minimal standard – managing to values will lead to durable success.

6. Meaning Over Mechanics

Most people would like to know their work has meaning.

The meaning may be in the work itself, in the values of the organization, or the pride people derive from working with friends and knowing they are good at what they do. In a radio interview, one NASA scientist talked about the meaning of her work as a spiritual journey into the universe and the mind of God. Martin Rosenblum, the Harley-Davidson historian, says he works for the company because it has 'soul' and describes the customization of bikes as 'As a sort of folk art ritual where the rider recreates the bike as an innovation of himself or herself.'[187]

How we view our work determines the extent to which it has meaning. Real-estate people can decide whether they want to 'sell houses' or help people 'find homes' and insurance salespeople can decide whether they are 'selling policies' or helping people 'protect their families.' People get frustrated if they think of what they're doing as 'just a job'; they are slightly more interested in 'work' but in every case the people who are outstanding see what they do as a 'calling,' the work has meaning.

Organizing for good means organizations understand they will be successful to the extent they treat employees as fully human and are interested in their hearts and minds as well as their arms and legs.

7. Manage Experiments Rather Than Make Decisions

Properly understood, the scientific method means executives manage experiments and keep looking for better ways to accomplish what they need to do.

This means effective executives manage an ongoing set of experiments to find better ways to serve people, rather than defending whatever approach they happen to be using at the moment. It means they are constantly adjusting what they do and how they do it in response to the many challenges described earlier.

In the end, we have returned to where we started. In 1911 Frederick Taylor's ideas represented a powerful application of ideas that led to significant improvements in all our lives. Now we need to move on.

Robert Hartman's ideas hold the potential to help ourselves and the organizations we have created become what they ought to be. The question is what each of us can do to become fully who we ought to be and develop organizations of which we are proud and respect.

Bibliography

Ackoff, Russell L. (1991). *Ackoff's Fables – Irreverent Reflections on Business and Bureaucracy*, New York: Wiley.

Allio, Robert J. and Pennington, Malcom W. (1979). *Corporate Planning*, New York: AMACOM.

American Heritage, (1972). *Great Stories of American Business*. New York: American Publishing Company, Inc.

Appelbaum, Richard P. (1970). *Theories of Social Change*. Chicago: Rand McNally College Publishing Company.

Argyris, Chris. (2000). *Flawed Advice and the Management Trap – How Managers Can Know When They Are Getting Good Advice and When They are Not*. Oxford: Oxford University Press.

Armstrong, Karen. (2005). *A Short History of Myth*. Edinburgh: Cannongate.

Augustine, Norman R. (1986). *Augustine's Laws*. New York: Viking Penguin, Inc.

Auletta, Ken. (1986). *Greed and Glory On Wall Street*. New York: Warner Books.

Auletta, Ken. (1991). *Three Blind Mice, How the TV Networks Lost Their Way*. New York: Random House.

Barber, William J. (1967). *A History of Economic Thought*. Middlesex: Penguin Books, Ltd.

Barker, Joel Arthur. (1985). *Discovering the Future: The Business of Paradigms*. St. Paul: I.L.I Press.

Barker, Joel Arthur, Future Edge, Discovering New Paradigms of Success, Morrow and Co., New York, 1992

Belasco, James A. (1990). *Teaching Elephants to Dance: Empowering Change in Your Organization*. New York: Crown Publishers.

Bell, Daniel. (1973). *The Coming of Post-Industrial Society.* New York: Basic Books, Inc.

Bell, Daniel and Kristol, Irving. (1981). *The Crisis In Economic Theory.* New York: Basic Books, Inc.

Bennis, Warren. (1993). *An Invented Life: Reflections on Leadership and Change*, Reading: Addison-Wesley Publishing Company.

Bennis, Warren. (1989). *On Becoming a Leader*. Reading: Addison-Wesley Publishing Company.

Bennis, Warren and Nanus, Burt. (1985). *Leaders*, New York: Harper & Row.

Bennis, Warren. (1989). *Why Leaders Can't Lead.* San Francisco: Jossey-Bass Publishers.

Berle, A.A. Jr. (1957) *Economic Power and the Free Society*. New York: Center for the Study of Democratic Institutions.

Berman, Morris.(1981). *The Reenchantment of the World.* New York: Bantam Books with Cornell University Press.

Beveridge, D.W. Jr. (1982). *The Yes Syndrome*, Barrington: D.W. Beveridge, Jr. and Associates.

Blanchard, Kenneth, Donald Carew, and Eunice Parisi-Carew. (1990). *The One Minute Manager - Builds High Performing Teams*. Escondido: Blanchared Training & Development.

Block, Peter. (1987). *The Empowered Manager*: Positive Political Skills At Work. San Francisco: Jossey-Bass Publishers.

Bloom, Allan. (1987). *The Closing of the American Mind.* New York: Simon and Schuster, Inc.

Bok, Sissela. (1989). *Lying: Moral Choice in Public and Private Life*. New York: Vintage Books.

Bolman, Lee G., and Deihl, Terrence. (1991). *Reframing Organizations*. San Francisco: Jossey Bass.

Boorstin, Daniel J. (1974). *Democracy and Its Discontents.* New York: Vintage Books.

Boorstin, Daniel J. (1974). *The Americans: The Democratic Experience.* New York: Vintage Books.

Botkin, James W. and Elmanjra, Mahdi and Malitza, Mircea. (1979). *No Limits To Learning.* Oxford: Pergamon Press.

Breyer, Stephen. (1993). *Breaking the Vicious Circle: Toward Effective Risk Regulation.* Cambridge: Harvard University Press.

Brown, Ray E. (1982). *Judgment in Administration.* Chicago: American College of Hospital Administrators.

Bucholz, Todd G. (1990). *New Ideas From Dead Economists.* New York: First Plume Printing.

Burns, James MacGregor. (1972). *Uncommon Sense.* New York: Harper & Row.

Burns, James MacGregor. (1978) *Leadership.* New York: Harper & Row.

Burrough, Bryan and Helyar, John, *Barbarians At the Gate: The Fall of RJR Nabisco*, Harper & Row, New York, 1990.

Bynam, William C. Ph.D. with Cox, Jeff. *Zapp! (1989).* Pittsburgh Development Dimensions International Press.

Byrum, C. Stephen. (1995). *The Value Structure of Theology.* Acton: Tapestry Press.

Callahan, Raymond E. (1962). *Education and the of Efficiency.* Chicago: The University of Chicago Press.

Campbell, Joseph. (1978). *Myths To Live By.* New York: Bantam Books.

Caplow, Theodore, Hicks, Louis, Wattenberg, Ben. (2000). *The First Measured Century, An Illustrated Guide to Trends in America.* Washington D.C.: AEI Press.

Capra, Fritjof. (1982). *The Turning Point.* Toronto: Bantam Books.

Carlzon, Jan. (1987). *Moments of Truth.* New York: , Ballinger Publishing.

Casale, Anthony M. with Lerman, Philip. (1986). *USA Today: Tracking Tomorrow's Trends.* Kansas City: Andrews, McMeel & Parker.

Casti, John L. (1989). *Paradigms Lost.* New York: William Morrow & Company, Inc.

Celente, Gerald with Milton, Tom. (1990). *Trend Tracking.* New York: John Wiley and Sons.

Cerf, Christopher and Navasky, Victor. (1984). *The Experts Speak.* New York: Pantheon Books.

Cetron, Marvin and O'Toole, Thomas. (1982). *Encounters With the Future.* New York: McGraw-Hill Book Company.

Chandler, Alfred D. Jr. (1962). *Strategy and Struggle: Chapters In the History of the American Industrial Enterprise.* Cambridge: The M.I.T. Press.

Chappel, Tom. (1993). *The Soul of a Business: Managing for Profit and the Common Good.* New York: Bantam Books.

Clifford, Donald J. Jr. and Cavanah, Richard E. (1985). *The Winning Performance.* Toronto: , Bantam Books.

Collins, James C. and Porrat, Jerry I. (1987). *Built to Last – Successful Habits of Visionary Companies.* New York: Harper Business.

Collins, James C. (2001). *Good to Great – Why Some Companies Make the Leap and Others Don't.* New York: Harper Business.

Comte-Sponville, Andre. (1986). *The Uses of Philosophy in Everyday Life. New York:* Henry Holt.

Covey, Stephen. (1989). *7 Habits of Highly Effective People – Powerful Lessons in Personal Change.* New York: Fireside.

Culbert, Samuel A., and McDonough, John J. (1985). *Radical Managerment—Power Politics and the Pursuit of Trust.* New York: The Free Press A Division of Macmillan, Inc.

Davis, Stanley M. (1987). *Future Perfect.* Reading: Addison-Wesley Publishing Company, Inc.

Deal, Terrence E. and Kennedy, Allan A. (1982). *Corporate Cultures.* Reading: Addison-Wesley Publishing Company.

Deming, W. Edward. (1982). *Out of the Crisis.* Cambridge: Massachusetts Institute of Technology.

DePree, Max. (1992). *Leadership Jazz.* New York: Currency Doubleday

DePree, Max. (1989). *Leadership Is An Art.* New York: Doubleday.

DeTocqueville, Alexis. (1945). *Democracy In America*. New York: Vintage Books.

Dibble, David. (2002). *The New Agreements in the Workplace – Releasing the Human Spirit.* New York: Emiritus Group.

Dorner, Dietrich. *The Logic of Failure: Why Things Go Wrong and What We Can Do to Make Them Right.* New York: Metropolitan Books, Henry Holt and Co.

Drucker, Peter F. (1966). *The Effective Executive.* New York: Harper & Row.

Drucker, Peter F. (1970). *The Future of Industrial Man.* New York: The New American Library of World Literature, Inc.

Drucker, Peter F. (1954). *The Practice of Management.* New York: Harper & Row.

Drucker, Peter F. (1989). *The New Realities.* New York: Harper & Row.

Drucker, Peter F. (1985). *Innovation and Entrepreneurship.* New York: Harper & Row.

Dyson, Freeman. (1988). *Infinite In All Directions.* New York: Harper & Row.

Eckerson, Wayne W. (2004). *Performance Dashboards.* New Jersey: Wiley.

Edwards, Rem. (2000). *Religious Values and Valuations.* Knoxville: Paidia.

Edwards, Rem and Davis, John W. (1991). *Forms of Value and Valuation.* Lanham: University Press of America.

Ellis, Arthur R. (1994). *Freedom to Live, - The Robert Hartman Story.* Amsterdam: Rodopi.

Etzioni, Amatai. (1988). *The Moral Dimension – Towards a New Economics*, New York: Free Press.

Fallows, James. (1996). *Breaking the News – How the Media Undermines American Democracy.* New York: Pantheon Books.

Feigenaum, Edward A. and McCorduck, Pamela. *The Fifth Generation.* Reading: Addison-Wesley.

Ferguson, Marilyn. (1980). *The Aquarian Conspiracy.* Los Angeles: J.P. Tarcher, Inc.

Forrester, Jay W. (1961). *Industrial Dynamics.*, Cambridge: The M.I.T. Press.
Foster, Richard. (1986). *Innovation: The Attacker's Advantage.* New York: Summit Books.
Foster, Timothy R V. (1993). *101 Great Mission Statements.* London: Kogan Page Limited.
Fox, Matthew. (1995). *The Reinvention of Work — A New Vision of Livelihood for Our Time.* San Francisco: Harper.
Frank, Robert H. (1988). *Passions Within Reason.* New York: W.W. Norton & Company.
Frankl, Viktor E. (1984). *Man's Search for Meaning — An Introduction to Logotherapy.* New York: Touchstone
Frankl, Viktor E. (2000). *Man's Search for Ultimate Meaning.* New York: Basic Books.
Gabor, Andrea. (2000). *The Capitalist Philosophers, - The Genius of Modern Business – Their Lives, Times and Ideas.* New York: Times Books.
Galbraith, John Kenneth. (1967). *The New Industrial State.* New York: New American Library.
Galbraith, John Kenneth. (1958). *The Affluent Society.* Boston: Houghton Mifflin Company.
Galbraith, John Kenneth. (1977). *The Age of Uncertainty.* Boston: Houghton Mifflin Company.
Gardner, John W. (1990) *On Leadership.* New York: The Free Press.
Gardner, John W. (1961). *Excellence* New York: Harper & Row.
Gardner, John W. (1968). *No Easy Victories.* NewYork: Harper & Row.
Gladwell, Malcolm. *Blink – The Power of Thinking Without Thinking.* New York: Little Brown and Company.
Gladwell, Malcolm. (2000). *The Tipping Point – How Little Things Make a Big Difference.* New York: Little Brown.
Gleick, James. (2003). *Isaac Newton.* New York: Pantheon Books.
Gleick, James, Faster – The Acceleration of Just About Everything, Pantheon, New York, 1999
Goldratt, Eliyaha M. and Cox, Jeff. (1986) *The Goal: A Process of*

Ongoing Improvement. Crotin-on-Hudson: North River Press, Inc.

Goleman, Daniel. (1995). *Emotional Intelligence.* New York: Bantam.

Greenleaf, Robert K. (1997). *Servant Leadership — A Journey Into the Nature of Legitimate Power and Greatness.* NewYork: Paulet Press.

Hammond, Sue Annis. (1998) *The Thin Book of Appreciative Inquiry.* Plano: Thin Book Publishing.

Handy, Charles. (1994). *The Age of Paradox.* Boston: Harvard Business School Press.

Handy, Charles. (1990). *The Age of Unreason.* Boston: Harvard Business School Press.

Harford, Tim. (2006). *The Undercover Economist.* Oxford: Oxford University Press.

Harris, Marvin. (1981) *Why Nothing Works—the Anthropology of Daily Life* (Originally published as *America Now).* New York: Touchstone.

Harris, Louis, *Inside America*, Vintage Books, New York, 1987.

Harris, Marvin, *America Now*, Simon and Schuster, Inc., New York, 1981.

Hartman, Robert. (1967). *The Structure of Value.* Carbondale: Southern Illinois University Press.

Harvard Business Review (1979). *Harvard Business Review - On Management.* New York: Harper & Row.

Harvard Business Review (1979). *Harvard Business Review - On Human Relations.* New York: Harper & Row.

Harvey, Jerry B. (1988). *The Abilene Paradox —and Other Meditations on Management.* Lexington: D.C. Heath and Company.

Hawken, Paul. (1987). *Growing A Business.* New York: Fireside Books.

Hawken, Paul. (1993). *The Ecology of Commerce – A Declaration of Sustainability.* New York: Harper Business.

Hawkings, Stephen W. (1988). *A Brief History of Time.* Toronton: Bantam Books.

Heider, John. (1985). *The Tao of Leadership*. Toronton: Bantam Books.

Herzberg, Joseph, Mausner, Baeernard, Snyderman, Barbara Bloch. *The Motivation to Work*. New York: Transaction Publishers, 7th Printing.

Himmelfarb, Gertrude. *The De-Moralization of Society – From Victorian Times to Modern Values*. New York: Vintage.

Hindrey, Leo. (2005). *It Takes a CEO*. New York: Free Press.

Hodges, Andrew. (1983). *Alan Turing: The Enigma*. New York: Simon and Schuster, Inc.

Horton, Thomas R. *The CEO Paradox - The Privilege and Accountability of Leadership*, New York: Amacom.

Howard, Phillip K. (1994). *The Death of Common Sense, How Law is Suffocating America*, New York: Warner Books.

Hughes, Robert. (1993) *Culture of Complaint—The Fraying of America*. New York: Oxford University Press

Jay, Anthony. (1971). *Corporate Man*. New York: Pocket Books.

Johnson, Spencer. (1998). *Who Moved My Cheese*, New York: Putman.

Juran, J.M. (1988). *Juran on Planning for Quality*. New York: The Free Press.

Kanigel, Robert. (1997). *The One Best Way – Frederick Winslow Turner and the Enigma of Efficiency*. New York: Penguin Books.

Kanter, Rosabeth Moss. (1983). *The Change Masters*. New York: Simon and Schuster, Inc.

Kanter, Rosabeth Moss. (1989). *When Giants Learn to Dance*. New York: Simon & Schuster.

Kelleher, William J. (2005). *Progressive Logic, Framing a Unified Theory of Values for Progressives*. La Jolla: Empathic Science Institute.

Kotter, John P. (1988) *The Leadership Factor*. New York: The Free Press.

Kouzes, James M. and Posner, Barry Z.. (1987) *The Leadership Challenge, How to Get Extraordinary Things Done in Organizations*. San Francisco: Jossey Bass.

Kriegel, Robert J. and Patler, Louis. *If it ain't broke. . .BREAK IT!*. New York: Warner Books.

Krames, Jeffrey A. (2004). *The Welch Way*. New York: McGraw Hill.

Kronman, Anthony T. *The Lost Lawyer: Failing Ideals of the Legal Profession*, Cambridge: The Belknap .

Kuhn, Thomas S. (1970). *The Structure of Scientific Revolutions*. Chicago: The University of Chicago Press.

Kuhn, Thomas S. (1979). *The Essential Tension*. Chicago: The University of Chicago Press.

Kurzweil, Ray. *The Singularity is Near – When Humans Transcend Biology*. New York: Viking.

Kurzweil, Ray. (1999). *The Age of the Spiritual Machine*. New York: Penguin.

Leonard, George B. (1960). *The Transformation – A Guide to the Inevitable Changes in Humankind*. New York: Bantam.

Lerner, Michael. *The Politics of Meaning – Restoring Hope and Possibility in an Age of Cynicism*. Reading: Addison Wesley.

Lewis, Hunter, with Foreward by M. Scott Peck. *A Question of Values: Six Ways We make the Personal Choices That Shape Our Lives*. San Francisco: Harper.

Levitt, Stephen D. and Dubner, Stephen J. (2005). *Freakenominics – A Rogue Economist Explores the Hidden Side of Everything*. New York: Morrow and Co.

Levitt, Theodore. (1986). *The Marketing Imagination*. New York: Free Press.

Lindaman, Edward B. and Lippitt, Ronald O. (1979) *Choosing the Future You Prefer*. Washington Development Publications.

Louv, Richard. (1983). *America II*, Los Angeles: Jeremy P. Tarcher, Inc.

Ludeman, Kate and Erlandson, Eddie. (2003). *Radical Change, Radical Results – 7 Actions to Become the Force for Change on Your Organization*. New York: Kaplan Business

Lutz, William. (1988). *DoubleSpeak*. New York: Harper & Row Publishers.

Maccoby, Michael. Why Work – Motivating and Leading the New Generation,

Machiavelli, Noccolo. (1961). *The Prince.* New York: Penguin.
Maxwell, John C. (2003). *Ethics 101.* New York: Center Street.
McGervey, John D. (1986). *Probabilities In Everyday Life.* New York: Ivy Books.
McGregor, Douglas. (1985). *The Human Side of the Enterprise – 25th Anniversary Printing.* New York: McGraw Hill.
McRae, Hamish. (1994). *The World in 2020: Power, Culture and Prosperity*, Boston: Harvard Business School Press.
Menand, Louis. (2001). *The Metaphysical Club.* New York: Farrar, Strauss Giroux.
Miller, Lawrence M. (1989). *Barbarians To Bureaucrats*, New York: Clarkson N. Potter, Inc.
Miller, Douglas T. and Nowak, Marion. (1977). *The Fifties: The Way We Really Were.* Garden City: Doubleday & Company, Inc.
Miller, Robert B. and Heiman, Stephen E. with Tad Tuleja, (1987). *Conceptual Selling.* Walnut Creek: Miller-Heiman Inc.
Mintzberg, Henry. *Managers, Not MBAs – A Hard Look at the Soft Practice of Managing and Management Development.* San Francisco: Barrett Kohler.
Mintzberg, Henry. (1994).*The Rise and Fall of Strategic Planning: Reconceiving Roles for Planning, Plans, Planners.* New York: The Free Press.
Morrison, Ian and Schmid, Greg. (1994). *Future Tenses —The Business of Realities of the Next Ten Years.* New York: William Morrow & Company.
Naisbitt, John. (1982). *Megatrends: Ten New Directions Transforming Our Lives*, New York: Warner Books.
Nanus, Burt. (1989). *The Leaders Edge: The Seven Keys to Leadership in a Turbulent World.* Chicago: Contemporary Books.
Norman, Donald A. (1988). *The Design of Everyday Things.* New York: Doubleday Currency.
Novak, Michael. (1996). *Business as a Calling – Work and the Examined Life.* New York: Free Press.
O' Hear, Anthony. *After Progress – Finding the Old Way*

Forward. New York: Bloomsbury.
O'Neill, Gerard K. (1983). *The Technology Edge.* New York: Simon and Schuster, Inc.
Osborne, David, and Gabbler, Ted. (1992). *Reinventing Government – How the Entrepreneurial Spirit is Transforming The Public Sector*. Reading: Addison
O'Toole, James. (1995). *Leading Change - The Argument for Values-Based Leadership.* New York: Ballantine Books.
Ohmae, Kenichi. (1982). *The Mind of the Strategist.* Middlesex: Penguin Books.
Ouchi, William. (1984). *The M-Form Society.* Reading: Addison-Wesley Publishing Company.
Ouchi, William G. (1981) *Theory Z: How American Business Can Meet the Japanese Challenge*. New York: Avon Books.
Parkinson, C. Northcote. (1957). *Parkinson's Law and Other Studies In Administration.* Boston: Houghton Mifflin Company..
Penzias, Arno. (1989). *Ideas and Information: Managing in a High-Tech World.* New York: W. W. Norton & Company.
Peters, Tom and Austin, Nancy. (1985). *A Passion for Excellence.* New York: Random House.
Peters, Tom. (1987). *Thriving On Chaos.* New York: Harper & Row.
Pfeiffer, J. William. (1989). *Shaping Strategic Planning.* Glenview: Scott, Foresman and Company.
Phillips, Kevin. (2006). *American Theocracy.* New York: Viking.
Poundstone, William. (1992). *Prisoner's Dilemma: John von Neumann, Game Theory, and the Puzzle of the Bomb.* New York: Doubleday.
Pomerory, Leon. *The New Science of Axiological Psychology.* Amsterdam: Value Inquiry Book Series.
Putnam, Robert. (2000). *Bowling Alone – The Collapse and Revival of American Community.* New York: Simon and Schuster.
Raphael, Adam. (1994). *Ultimate Risk: The Inside Story of the Lloyd's Catastrophe.* New York: Bantam Press.

Sampson, Anthony. (1981). *The Money Lenders.* New York: The Viking Press. 1981.

Scherkenbach, William W. *The Deming Route To Quality and Productivity.* Washington D.C: CEEPress Books.

Schnaars, Steven P. (1989). *Megamistakes.* New York: The Free Press.

Schumacher, E. F. (1973). *Small is Beautiful.* New York: Harper & Rowe Publishing.

Schwartz, Peter. (2003). *Inevitable Surprises.* New York: Gotham Books.

Selbourne, David. *The Principle of Duty.* London: Sinclair Stevenson.

Senge, Peter M. (1990). *The Fifth Discipline.* New York: Doubleday Currency.

Shook, Robert L. (1980). *The Entrepreneurs.* New York: Barnes and Noble Books.

Shurkin, Joel. (1985). *Engines of the Mind.* New York: Pocket Books.

Skidelsky, Robert. (1983). *John Meynard Keynes – Hopes Betrayed, 1883-1920.* New York: Penguin.

Smith, Douglas K. and Alexander, Robert C. (1988) *Fumbling the Future*, New York: William Morrow and Company, Inc.

Snow, C.P. (1993). *The Two Cultures.* Cambridge: Cambridge University Press.

Sobel, Robert. (1981). *IBM Colossus In Transition.* Toronto: Bantam Books.

Speer, Albert. (1970). *Inside the Third Reich – Memoirs.* New York: Touchstone.

Starr, Paul. (1982). *The Social Transformation of American Medicin.* New York: Basic Books, Inc.

Stewart, James B. (1991). *Den of Thieves.* New York: Simon and Schuster.

Taleb, Nassim Nicholas. (2005). *Fooled by Randomness – The Hidden Role of Chance in the Markets and in Life.* New York: Random House.

Tannen, Deborah, Ph.D. (1990) *You Just Don't Understand:*

Women and Men in Conversation. New York: Morrow Books.

Tapscott, Don. (1996). *The Digital Economy — Promise and Peril in the Age of Networked Intelligence.* New York: McGraw-Hill.

Taylor, Frederick Winslow (1998). *The Principles of Scientific Management.* Mineola: Dover Publications.

Taylor, Harold L. (1984) *Delegate: The Key to Successful Management.* New York: Warner Books Inc.

Theobold, Robert. (1992). *Turning the Century: Personal and Organizational Strategies for Your Changed World.* Indianapolis: Knowledge Systems Inc.

Thurow, Lester C. (1985) *The Zero-Sum Solution.* New York: Simon and Schuster, Inc.

Thurow, Lester C. (1983). *Dangerous Currents.* New York: Random House. 1983.

Thurow, Lester C. (1980). *The Zero-Sum Society.* Middlesex: Penguin Books.

Tichy, Noel M. and Devanna, Mary Anne. (1987) *The Transformational Leader*, New York: John Wiley & Sons.

Toffler, Alvin and Heidi Toffler. (1990). *Power Shift: Knowledge, Wealth, and Violence at the Edge of the 21st Century.* New York: Bantam Books.

Tregoe, Benjamin B. and Zimmerman, John W. (1980). *Top Management Strategy*, New York: Touchstone Book.

Tregoe, Benjamin B. Zimmerman, John W., Smith, Ronald A., Tobia, Peter M. *Vision and Action: Putting A Winning Strategy to Work.* New York: Simon & Schuster, Inc.

Urdang, Laurence, Editor. (1996). *Timetables of History, Updated Edition.* New York: Simon and Schuster.

von Hippel, Eric, (1988). *The Sources of Innovation.* New York: Oxford University Press.

von Oech, Roger. (1986). *A Kick In the Seat of the Pants.* New York: Harper & Row.

von Oech, Roger. (1983). *A Whack On the Side of the Head.* New York: Warner Books, Inc.

Wallis, Jim. (1994). *The Soul of Politics: A Practical and*

Prophetic Vision of Change. Mary Knoll: The New Press.

Walton, Mary. (1986). *The Deming Management Method.* New York: The Putnam Publishing Group.

Waterman, Robert H. Jr. (1987). *The Renewal Factor.* Toronto: Bantam Books.

Weaver, Paul H. (1988). *The Suicidal Corporation.* New York: Simon and Schuster, Inc.

Weiner, Edie, and Brown, Arnold. *FutureThink, How to Think Clearly in a Time of Change.* New York: Pearson/Prestiss Hall.

Weisbord, Marvin R and Janoff, Sandra. *Future Search — An Action Guide to Finding Common Ground in Organizations and Communities.* San Francisco: Berrett-Koehler Publishers.

Wheatley, Margaret J. (1992). *Leadership and the New Science.* San Francisco: Berrett-Koehler Publishers Inc.

Whyte, David. (2001) *Crossing the Unknown Sea – Work as a Pilgrimage of Identity.* New York: Riverhead Books.

Whyte, David. (1994). *The Heart Aroused – Poetry and the Preservation of the Soul In Corporate America.* New York: Doubleday.

Whyte, William H. Jr. (1956) *The Organization Man.* Garden City: Doubleday Anchor Books.

Will, George F, (1990). *Suddenly - The American Idea Abroad and At Home 1986-1990.* New York: The Free Press.

Will, George F. (1990). *Men At Work: The Craft of Baseball.* New York: Macmillan Publishing Company.

Willens, Harold. (1994). *The Trimtab Factor.* New York: William Morrow and Company, Inc.

Wilson, Edward O. (1998). *Consilience.* New York: Knopf.

Wilson, James Q. (1989). *Bureaucracy - What Government Agencies Do and Why they Do It.* New York: Basic Books.

Wilson, Robert A., Editor. *Character Above All*, New York: Simon and Schuster.

Winston, Stephanie. (1983). *The Organized Executive.* New York: Warner Books.

Wishy, Bernard. (1968). *The Child and the Republic.* Philadelphia: University Press.

Wrege, Charles D. and Greenwood, Ronald D. (1991). *Frederick W. Taylor, The Father of Scientific Management, Myth and Reality*. Burr Ridge: Irwin.

Zuboff, Shoshana. (1984). *In the Age of the Smart Machine.* New York: Basic Books, Inc.

Zukav, Gary. (1989). *The Seat of the Soul.* New York: Simon and Schuster, Inc. 1989.

Zukav, Gary. (1979). *The Dancing Wu Li Masters.* Toronto: Bantam Books.

Endnotes and Comments

Introduction

[1] Kanigel, Robert, (1997). The One Best Way: Frederick Winslow Taylor and the Enigma of Efficiency. New York, New York: Little, Brown and Co., page 11.
[2] Ibid, page 5
[3] Ibid, page 4
[4] Letter from Upton Sinclair, The Gospel of Efficiency, from papers in the Taylor Collection at Stevens Institute, Hoboken, New Jersey
[5] Taylor, Frederick W. (1911). The Principles of Scientific Management. Introduction, page IV
[6] Scenes from The Reinvention, Today's Companies Won't Make It, And Gary Hamel Knows Why, Fortune Magazine, September 4, 2000 page 386
[7] Whitney, John (1994) The Trust Factor: Liberating Profits and Restoring Corporate Vitality, New York, New York: McGraw Hill, Preface by Edwards Deming

Chapter One: Frederick Taylor and Scientific Management

The following materials have been helpful in understanding Frederick Taylor and his work. Of particular value is the Robert Kanigel biography, *The One Best Way: Frederick W. Taylor and the Enigma of Efficiency*. Other helpful books include *Taylorism Transformed:*

Scientific Management Since 1945 by Stephen Waring, *Frederick W. Taylor: The Father of Scientific Management : Myth and Reality* by Charles D. Wrege, Ronald G. Greenwood, Daniel Nelson's *Frederick W. Taylor and the Rise of Scientific Management* and sections of *Movers and Shakers – the 100 Most Influential Thinkers in Modern Business.* There is also a video, *Stopwatch,* produced for KQED Public Television.

In addition, the Frederick W. Taylor collection at the S.C. Williams Library at Stevens Institute was a valuable source of information. The collection includes many of Taylor's papers and letters as well as copies of articles written about him and his work. Notable among these is the paper Shop Management written in 1903 as well as Taylor's typed notes of his work including personally typed job descriptions referenced in the book. Doris Oliver and the library staff were especially helpful with my work at the library.

[8] Galbraith, John Kenneth. (1958). *The Affluent Society*, New York: Houghton Miflin.
[9] Hacker, Andrew. (1987, March 2). The Best of Times in the USA. Fortune, page 136
[10] Menand, Louis. (2001). *The Metaphysical Club.* New York: Farrar Strauss Giroux. preface, page X
[11] The gunfight at the OK Corral took place on October 26, 1881
[12] See, for example, Goldman, Steven L. Science in the 20th Century: A Social-Intellectual History, Chantilly: The Teaching Company.
[13]Menand, Louis. In the Introduction Menand discusses Holmes and his colleagues' view of ideas. Ideas, they believed, were like 'tools' that enable people to cope; they were social in nature; they had to be adaptable to survive, and they should never become ideologies. page 65
[14] Irons, Peter. (2003) *The History of the Supreme Court.* Chantilly: The Teaching Company.
[15] Menand. Agassiz's 'students were required to observe first and construct generalizations later.' pages 100-101.
[16] There are numerous sources for dates and events. These specific examples came from www.delmar.edu/scosci and www.inventors.about.com
[17] Collected Papers, Frederick W. Taylor Collection, Samuel C. Williams Library

---

[18] Taylor. page 35,
[19] Ibid. Introduction, page iv
[20] Ibid. Introduction, page iv
[21] Ibid. page 9
[22] Ibid. page 15
[23] The original movie starred Clifton Webb, Jeanne Crain and Myrna Loy. There was a remake in 2003 and *Cheaper by the Dozen 2* was released in 2005.
[24] Taylor. page 27.
[25] Ibid. page 31. Taylor's data on shoveling and how to do it is spelled out is good example of his thoroughness.
[26] Ibid. page 43,44
[27] Ibid. page 55.
[28] Rivlin, Gary. (2004, December 19). Who's Afraid of China? New York Times, Section 3, page 1
[29] Ordonez, Jennifer. (2000, May19). Next! An Efficiency Drive: Fast Food Lanes Are Getting Even Faster. Wall Street Journal, page 1
[30] Hays, Constance I. (2004, November 14). What Wal-Mart Knows About Customers' Habits, New York Times, page 1
[31] There are numerous sources of these statistics. These came from http://sports.espn.go.com/golf/statistics
[32] Shatz, Aaron. (2004, January 12). 'Tis Better to Have Rushed and Lost Than Never to Have Rushed at All. Football Outsiders. footballoutsiders.com
[33] John Deere web site product descriptions.
[34] Rivlin, Gary. (2006, August 13).Wine Ratings May Not Pass the Sobriety Test. New York Times, page 13
[35] Taylor, page 21
[36] Taylor, page 17
[37] Taylor, page 9 and 10, page 18
[38] Taylor page 33
[39] Kanigel, page 187
[40] Taylor, page 21
[41] Chen, Rosita S. and Pan, Sheng-Der. (1980) Frederick Taylor's Contributions to Accounting. The Accounting Historians Journal. Vol. 7. No. 1.
[42] Kanigel, 269
[43] Kanigel, 269

[44] Tom Peter's company - Center for Management Excellence - conducts these intensive four-day seminars for top management - known to alumni as 'Skunk Camps'
[45] Kanigel 430-431
[46] From the Taylor Collection, New York Times, (1910). Nov. 22.
[47] Conversion Factors, Consumer Price Index, Robert C. Sahr, Oregon State University
[48] Callahan, Raymond E. (1964) Education and the Cult of Efficiency, Chicago: University of Chicago Press. Pages 71-75.
[49] Whonamedit.com. Codman applied the 'end result system' to his hospital. The idea of a hospital register to help physicians improve the quality of care they deliver had been presented in 1803 by the British physician Sir Thomas Percival (1740-1804).
[50] Kanigel, page 523-524
[51] Kanigel page 13
[52]National Center for Health Statistics web site. http://www.cdc.gov/nchs/howto/w2w/w2welcom.htm
[53] Social Security web page. www.ssa.gov
[54] National Center for Educational Statistics
[55] Kelly, Kevin. (2005). Wired Magazine. Issue 13.08.
[56] Naisbitt, John. (1982) *Megatrends*. New York City: Warner Books
[57]Tapscott, Dan and Caston, Art. (1992) *Paradigm Shift: The New Promise of Information Technology*, New York City: McGraw Hill
[58] Wheatley, Margaret. 1999. *Leadership and the New Science: Discovering Order in a Chaotic World* (Revised), San Francisco, California; Barrett-Kohler.
[59] Osborne, David and Gabler, Ted. (1992). *Reinventing Government: How the Entrepreneurial Spirit Is Transforming the Public Sector.* Boston: Addison Wesley.
[60] Handy, Charles. (1990). *The Age of Unreason.* Cambridge: Harvard University Press.
[61] Glenn, Joshua. (1995). Sociology on the Skids, Utne Reader, November-December, In Brief, page 28
[62] Leanne Kaiser Carlson, the health care futurist, has made this point in conversations and presentations for several years.
[63] Hollowell, Edward M. (2005). Overloaded Circuits, Harvard Business Review, January

[64] Gullapalli, Diya. (2005, May 4). Audit Profession Feels Squeeze, Wall Street Journal, p. C1
[65] Schwartz, John. (2004, Sept. 5).) Always on the Job, Employees Pay with Health, New York Times.
[66] Labich, Kenneth. (1995, Jan.20). Kissing Off, Fortune Magazine.
[67] Friskics-Warren, Bill. (2002, Aug. 25).The Dixie Chicks Keep the Heat on Nashville, New York Times, Arts and Leisure p. 1

Chapter Two: Robert Hartman and Axiology

The chapter draws on *The Structure of Value, Freedom to Live: The Robert Hartman Story*, Edited by Arthur R. Ellis, *Forms of Value and Valuation* by Dr. Rem Edwards and John W. Davis, several of Hartman's papers including the "Individual in Management', 'Theory and Practice in Industrial Relations', Ethics and Economics: The Moral Basis of Industrial Relations', "Life and Entropy", "The Science of Decision-Making", "The Scientific Method of Analysis and Synthesis", articles and materials drawn from his papers at the Hoskins Library at the University of Tennessee. It also draws on the work of The Hartman Institute and its members.

[68] After World War II Viktor Frankl Frankel wrote *Man's Search for Meaning* in 1946 documenting his experiences in the concentration camps.
[69] Individual in Management, p. 1
[70] Ibid. p. 26 and 27
[71] Ibid. p. 34
[72] Ibid. p. 26
[73]The case centered on Otto Ernst Remer, then an army major commanding the Berlin Guard Regiment, who was ordered by General von Hase (a co-conspirator) to arrest Dr. Goebbels, propaganda minister and Gauleiter of Berlin. Remer did as he was told. When the plot failed he was arrested and tried for treason. Hartman's point was if the plot had succeeded Remer would have been hailed as a hero. It was this example of the law as a vehicle for determining what was legal and not legal rather than what was right or wrong that lead to Hartman's desire to find another way to organize for good.

---

[74] Rita Hartman's report of her husband's nomination for the Nobel Prize can not be confirmed. The Nobel Prize nomination records are sealed for fifty years.
[75] Individual in Management, page 8
[76] Ibid. p. 62
[77] Ibid. p. 14
[78] The Greenleaf Center for Servant Leadership states servant leadership 'begins with the natural feeling that one wants to serve first, then conscious choice brings one to aspire to lead . . . The difference manifests itself in the care taken by the servant – first to make sure that other people's highest priorities are being served.' Greenleaf Center, www.greenleaf.org
[79] McGregor, Douglas. (2006). *The Human side of the Enterprise, Annotated Edition.* New York: McGraw Hill
[80] Private Westrend Group company data.
[81] Dunlap, Al. (1996) *Mean Business: How I Save Bad Companies and Make Good Companies Great.* New York: Frieside To further make his point Dunlap entitled one chapter 'Rambo in Pinstripes'.
[82] Byrne, John A. (1999, Oct. 18). *Chainsaw: The Notorious Career of Al Dunlap in the Era of Profit-at-Any-Price*, Business Week Online. Excerpt from Byrne's book. New York: Harper Books
[83] Edwards, Rem and Davis, John. (1991) *Forms of Value and Valuation*, New York: University Press of America. page 194
[84] Hartman Nationwide Presentation paper
[85] The Myers Briggs Foundation states 'The purpose of the Myers-Briggs Type Indicator® (MBTI) personality inventory is to make the theory of psychological types described by C. G. Jung understandable and useful in people's lives."
[86] The DISC Profile is based on the 1928 work of William Moulton Marston. It is a personality behavioral testing profile using a four dimensional model of normal behavior: dominance, influence, steadiness and conscientiousness.
[87] Goleman, Daniel (2006) *Emotional Intelligence 10th Anniversary Edition.* New York: Bantam Books
[88] The Hartman Value Profile assesses approximately sixty value tendencies including, for example, how we value work, our responsiveness to change, our tolerance and ability to deal with people among them.

---

[89] Papers in the Hartman collection at the University of Tennessee include copies of correspondence between Hartman and Maslow.

[90] Pico della Mirandola's "Oration on the Dignity of Man", Pico's central argument was "You, with no limit or no bound, may choose for yourself the limits and bounds of your nature."

[91] Kirkegaard, Soren. (1986) *Fear and Trembling.* New York: Penguin Calssics.

[92] Bennis, Warren G. and Thomas, Robert J. (2002, Sept.). Crucibles of Leadership, HBR At Large, Harvard Business Review. p. 39

[93] Hartman's discussion of sensitive people focused more explicitly on his wife and his belief that women were more sensitive than men.

[94]Warranty Week, (2006, June 16). Retrieved http://www.warrantyweek.com

[95] Editorial. Another Black Eye for H&R Block, New York Times, March 18, 2006

Chapter Three People: Organizing for Good

[96] Speer, Albert. (1970). *Inside the Third Reich*, Translated by Richard and Clara Winston. New York: Simon and Schuster.

[97] Ibid. p. 31

[98] Ibid, p. 21-32

[99] Ibid, page 500

[100] Ibid, page 32

[101] Ibid, Page 345

[102] Whyte, William H. (1956). *The Organization Man.* New York: Anchor Books.

[103] Katz, Ellen Florian. (2004, Dec. 13).The Gray Flannel Office, Fortune Magazine. p. 152 -160

[104] Ibid

[105] Hartman, page 6

[106] Graham, Jefferson. 2006, Jan 25). Jobs has Knack for Getting His Way. p. 3B

[107] Bilger, Burkhard . (2005, Sept. 5). The Egg Men, The New Yorker. p. 79

[108] Howard, Theresa. (2006, Jan. 24). Nike Replaces CEO After 13 Months. USA Today. p. 3b

---

[109] Herzberg, Frederick, Mausner, Bernard, Snyderman, Barbara Bloch Barbara Bloch. (1959). *The Motivation to Work*, New York: John Wiley. Introduction page xiii

[110] The additional factors Herzberg and his colleagues identified were the possibility of growth, interpersonal relationships, status, company policy and administration, working conditions, personal life, and job security

[111] Herzberg. (2002) "One More Time: How Do You Motivate Employees?" Harvard Business Review.

[112] Elton Mayo conducted the Hawthorne Experiments between 1927 and 1932 at the Western Electric Plant in Cicero, Illinois.

[113] The phrase had come from its use by sailors working on ships that transported soldiers. The sailors had tasks and were busy throughout the day. The soldiers being transported had nothing to do so they spent most of the day sitting around. In the work place soldiering, in Taylor's view, was a lack of effort predicated on the worker keeping his knowledge about how much could actually be accomplished from the manager.

[114] Taylor. p. 7. Kanigel. p. 214

[115] Brandeis, Louis. (1912) Business – A Profession. Commencement Address., Brown University. Retrieved from Babson College web site. http://roger.babson.edu/ethics/business2.htm

[116] O'Brien, Timothy. (2006, Mar.29). Up the Down Staircase - Why Do So Few Women Reach the Top of Big Law Firms?. New York Times, Section 3, p. 1. See also Rickleen, Lauren Stiller. (2006) Ending the Gauntlet, Removing the Barriers to Women's Success in Law, Thomson Legalworks,

[117] Fallows, James. (1996) *Breaking the News: How the Media Undermines American Democracy*. New York City, New York. Random House

[118] Walsh, Mary Williams. (2005, July 31). How Wall Street Wrecked United's Pension, New York Times, Section 3, p. 1

[119] Guyon, Janet. (2005, May 16). Jack Grubman Is Back. Just Ask Him. Fortune Magazine, p. 119

[120] Swidey, Neil (2004, Mar. 21). What Went Wrong?, Boston Globe,

[121] Emshwiller, John B. and McWilliams, Gary. (2006, Mar.29). Fastow is Grilled at Enron Trial. Wall Street Journal, p. 1

[122] Morgenstern, Gretchen. (2005, Dec 18). The Boss Actually Said This: Pay Me Less, New York Times, Section 3, p. 1

[123] Leonard, Devin and Elkind, Peter. All I Want is an Unfair Advantage. A Fortune Investigation. Fortune Magazine, p. 76
[124] Elkind, Peter. (2004, Oct.18). The Fall of the House of Grasso. Fortune Magazine, p. 284
[125] Benis, Warren and O' Toole, James. (2005, May). How Business Schools Lost Their Way. Harvard Business Review, p. 96
[126] Keillor, Garrison numerous web sites with copies of his quotes
[127] Kronman, Anthony. (1993). *The Lost Lawyer*, Cambridge: Harvard University Press.
[128] Ibid. page 2
[129] Ibid.
[130] Covey, Stephen, (1992). *Principle Centered Leadership*, New York: Free Press.
[131] Bennis, Warren. (1989). *On Becoming a Leader*. Perseus Publishing. Boston, Massachusetts
[132] Mehta, Zubin. (2001, Feb 5) Quote of the Day, New York Times Electronic Edition.
[133] Burns, James MacGregor. (1982). *Leadership*, New York: Harper Perennial.
[134] Collins, Jim. (2001, Jan.). Level 5 Leadership, Harvard Business Review, p. 67.
[135] O' Toole, James. (1995) *Leading Change*. San Francisco, California. Jossey Bass
[136] Wheatley, Margaret. (2006 Edition) *Leadership and the New Science: Discovering Order in a Chaotic World*. San Francisco: Berrett Kohler
[137] Charan, Ram and Bossidy, Larry. (2002) Execution: The Discipline of Getting Things Done. New York: Crown
[138] Porter, Michael E. (1996). What Is Strategy?. Harvard Business Review, pp Vol. 74. Number 6. Pp. 61 - 78
[139] Mintzberg's Ten Schools include: The Design School, The Planning School, The Positioning School, The Entrepreneurial School, The Cognitive School, The Learning School, The Power School, The Cultural School, The Environmental School, and The Configuration School.
[140] Zalesnick, Abraham. (1977, Jan.) Managers and Leaders: Are They Different?. Cambridge: Harvard Business Review.
[141] Kotter, John. (1999) *What Leaders Really Do*. Cambridge: Harvard Business School Press.

Chapter Four – Organizing for Good

[142] Taylor, p. 225
[143] Hartman. Nationwide paper, 105
[144] Shireman, Bill. (2003, Mar. 19). Email. Global Futures.
[145] Lutz, William. (1990). *Doublespeak.* New York: Harper Collins
[146] Fritsch, Jane. (2000, Sept. 17). Tales From the Dark Side of Golf, New York Times, p. WK 2
[147] Johnson, Peter. (2006, Aug 31). CBS Puts Couris on a digital diet. USA Today, p. 3D 2006
[148] The Year in Business, Fortune Magazine, December 24, 2001, p. 140
[149] Goofs|Glitches|Gotchas, Consumer Reports, September 2006, p. 63
[150] Willing, Richard. (2006, Mar. 31). Errors Prompt States to Watch Over Crime Labs, USA Today, p. 3A
[151] Beam, Alex. (2006, Aug.7). First, The Big Debacle, Fortune Magazine, August 7, 2006, page 22, Brooke Donald, Several Spots in Big Dig unsound, Governor says, USA Today, July 18, 2006, page 3A.
[152] Moore, Thomas. (1992). *Care of the Soul.* New York: Harper Collins
[153] Whyte, David. (2001). *Crossing the Unknown Sea.* New York, New York. Riverhead Books - busyness
[154] Thinkexist.com. Peter Senge quotes
[155] Morrison, Robert, Erickson, Tamara and Dychwald, Ken. (2006, Mar.). Managing Middlescence, Harvard Business Review, p. 79.
[156] Overman, Pat. (2006). 2006 Employee Opinion Survey, St. Bernard's Health. St. Bernard's received an "Employer of Choice" Award in part because of the ability of its managers to stay focused on the meaning of what they do.
[157] Each of these is an actual example of what some friends do. Each of us knows of countless others.
[158] Clark, Bruce. Valley Baptist Board Retreat 2004
[159] Bellis, Bellis. About: Inventions, Inventors of the Modern Computer, J. Presper Eckert and John Mauchly
[160] The Rubber Meets the Road, Consumer Reports, September 2005, page 9
[161] Pagels, Heinz. (1989) *The Dreams of Reason: The Computer and the Rise of the Sciences of Complexity.* New York, New York. Bantam
[162] Silberman, Steve. (2006, Jan.) Don't Even Think About Lying, Wired Magazine, p. 140

---

[163] Kurzweil, Ray. (1999) *The Age of Spiritual Machines: When Computers Exceed Human Intelligence*, New York: Penguin. *The Singularity Is Near :When Humans Transcend Biology*. (2006)
[164] Kurzweil, Ray. (1999, Nov.). Spiritual Machines: The Merging of Man and Machine, The Futurist, p.16.
[165] Joy, Bill. (2000,Apr.). Why the future doesn't need us. Wired Magazine
[166] Krebs, Michelle. (2002, Aug. 23.). Bells and Whistles, Wipers that know what to do, New York Times.
[167] Davis, Joshua (2006, July) Here Fishy, Fishy, Fishy, Wired Magazine, p. 32.
[168] Bureau of Legislative Research, Arkansas State Legislature
[169] Auletta, Ken. (1991) *Three Blind Mice: How the TV Networks Lost Their Way*. New York, New York. Random House, pages 332 through 334
[170] Allen, Laura. (2006, May). Science Confirms the Obvious, Popular Science, Retrieved on web site.
[171] Hartman, p. 107 Nationwide Paper on Management
[172] Collins, Jim. (1994) Introduction. Built to Last. New York, New York. HarperCollins.
[173] McGregor, Jena. FastCompany.com. Issue 86, September 2004. p. 85
[174] Occam's Law, The principle developed by William of Occam that "Entities should be not multiplied unnecessarily." Occam went further to state "We are to admit no more causes of natural things than such as are both true and sufficient to explain their appearance."
[175] People and Discoveries, A Science Odyssey, Public Broadcasting Corporation web site
[176] Roth, Daniel. (2005, Dec. 12). Quoted Often, Rarely Followed, Fortune Magazine, p.151
[177] National Defense University, Strategic Leadership and Decision-Making, 15, Values and Ethics, Retrieved on the web
[178] Ripley, Amanda. (2005, Oct. 31). How the Coast Guard gets it Right, Time Magazine, p. 50
[179] Gunther, Marc. (2004, Nov. 15). Money and Morals at GE, Fortune Magazine, p. 176
[180] O'Driscoll, Patrick. (2006, June 23). Denver Bookstore Makes Its Move, USA Today, p. 3A
[181] Tattered Cover web site.

[182] Lynch, David J. (2006, July 24) Thanks to its CEO, UPS Doesn't Just Deliver, USA Today, p. B1

[183] The Land-Grant College Act of 1862, Introduced by Justin Smith Morrill of Vermont, provided funding for institutions of higher learning in each state.

[184] Fluckinger, Don. The eBay Effect, Antiques Roadshow Insider, Volume 5, Number 1, January 2005. By any measure eBay has been extraordinarily successful with 114,000,000 registered users in nations around the world trading products in 50,000 categories containing 2,9000,000 items with sellers adding 3,500,000 new items each day and trading them at the rate of 1,020 each second.

[185] Kirkpatrick, David. (2006, Sept. 18) 'This has been a wake up call for us", Interview with Michael Dell, Fortune Magazine, p. 78

[186] Farrell, Greg. (2006, Sept. 28). Bad Harvard grads are poster boys for ethics classes, USA Today, p. 4B

[187] Lisa Matthews, Peering Inside the Bike Builder Brain, Discovery Channel web site

Printed in the United States
129752LV00005B/206/A

9 781432 715854